CHILDREN'S JUKEBOX

A SUBJECT GUIDE TO

Musical Recordings and Programming Ideas for Songsters Ages One to Twelve

Rob Reid

American Library Association
Chicago and London
1995

Cover and illustrations by Jan Jones-Smith

Text design and composition by Dianne M. Rooney in Stone Serif
using QuarkXpress 3.3 for the Power Macintosh 7100/66

Printed on 50-pound Glatfelter, a pH-neutral stock, and bound in
10-point C1S cover stock by McNaughton & Gunn, Inc.

The paper used in this publication meets the minimum requirements
of American National Standard for Information Sciences—Permanence
of Paper for Printed Library Materials, ANSI Z39.48-1992. ∞

Library of Congress Cataloging-in-Publication Data
Reid, Rob.
    Children's jukebox : a subject guide to musical recordings and
programming ideas for songsters ages 1 to 12 / Rob Reid.
        p.   cm.
    Includes bibliographical references (p.   ).
    Videography: p.
    ISBN 0-8389-0650-8
    1. Children's songs—Discography—Indexes.   2. Children's
songs—Reviews.   3. Children's libraries—Activity programs.
I. Title.
ML156.4.C5R45   1995
016.78242' 083' 0266—dc20   95-6163

Printed in the United States of America.

99   98   97   96   95   5   4   3   2   1

Dedicated to my loving family—
Jayne, Laura, Julia, Alice,
and Sam

♪ Contents ♪

Contents

Short Takes

Goodbye Songs   167

Songs Listed by Special Type

Appendixes

Acknowledgments

Thanks to Colleen Hannafin for her wonderful support, for her impressive contacts in the children's music industry, for sharing her huge collection of children's recordings, and for being such a good friend; Bruce, David, and Roxanne for the hours of shop talk; Joanne Tuller of the Children's Music Network for her detective work; David Downs-Reid and Shu Cheng for their help with the foreign language lists; the staff of the L. E. Phillips Memorial Public Library in Eau Claire, Wisconsin; editor Herb Bloom for steering this project in the right direction; Art Plotnik of the American Library Association for his support and guidance; Dr. Eric Kimmel for his advice and encouragement; my beat-up Sanyo tape recorder, now on its last legs, for the hundreds of hours of listening pleasure and research; my Mac Performa 550 for doubling as word processor and compact disc player; and most of all to my family for putting up with the piles of recordings around the house and my annoying habit of breaking into a children's song on any and every occasion.

♩♪ *Permissions* ♩♪

The author gratefully acknowledges permission to use the following:

Partial lyrics of "Won't You Be My Partner" © Emma O'Brien, 1989.

Partial lyrics of "I Love Mud," written by Rick Charette, © 1985 Pine Point Publishing (ASCAP).

Partial lyrics of "I'm a 3-Toed, Triple-Eyed, Double-Jointed Dinosaur" by Barry Louis Polisar from the audio release OLD DOGS, NEW TRICKS.

Partial lyrics to the song "Love Grows One by One" used with permission of Carol Johnson © 1981 Noeldner Music BMI, P.O. 6351, Grand Rapids, MI 49516. From the recording "Might As Well Make It Love"

Selection from "The Mother Song," words and music by David Stoeri © 1987.

"Late Last Night" by Joe Scruggs © 1984 Educational Graphics Press, Inc. Used by permission. All Rights Reserved.

Partial lyrics of "The Kindergarten Wall" by John McCutcheon. Copyright 1988 John McCutcheon/Appalsongs (ASCA) from *Mail Myself to You* (Rounder Records 8016)

"I Am a Pizza" from the recording "WHA'D' YA WANNA DO?" © 1983 BMI, Moose School Music, written by Peter Alsop.

Lyrics from "Heading On Down to the Barn" © 1991 Smilin' Atcha Music. Written by Kathy and Red Grammer, ISBN 1-886146-03-9

♩♪ *Introduction* ♩♪

Whew! What a fun project! I can't begin to add up the total number of hours spent listening to children's recordings for this work. Nearly 500 musical recordings were analyzed and enjoyed. Approximately 300 of those recordings made their way into this book.

Children's musical recordings are often overlooked as sources of ideas for classrooms and library programs. The 300 recordings included in this project were selected for their programming potential for preschool and elementary school-age children and the adults who serve them. This book was designed for classroom teachers, music teachers, librarians, early childhood instructors, children's performers, counselors, parents, and other adults interested in sharing music with young children.

The project started at the L. E. Phillips Memorial Public Library in Eau Claire, Wisconsin, where I serve as Children's Librarian. I had often used programming ideas from children's recordings for my library story programs and for my freelance children's entertainment business. While conducting programs and workshops, I realized many adults go no further than the picture book section of the library for their programming source. At that point, I started to make a special effort to share children's recordings with my colleagues. Many of these teachers and librarians then began to ask for recorded songs that fit specific themes. My staff and I had to rely on our personal experiences and memories to come up with titles, since no subject reference index on children's recorded music was available. *Voila*—the *Children's Jukebox* was born. Five years and hundreds of listening hours later, the final project is now in print.

The recordings included in this book had to meet certain criteria: (1) they had to be available for purchase from at least one national distributor of children's recorded music; (2) some of the songs included on the individual recordings had to fall under one of the thirty-five subject listings identified as popular themes for story programs and classroom use; (3) they had to pass extremely subjective yet rigorous "kid-testing" applications among my own children and those I serve at the public library. My favorite group of kid-testers (and mom-testers, dad-testers, and grandparent-testers) are those who show up at our library's monthly Family Storytime. I frequently (and affectionately) refer to them as "my guinea pigs" while trying yet another new song on them.

Recordings not used in this project included all-movement or all-exercise recordings, holiday recordings, and lullaby recordings. (A few lullaby recordings, however, were included because they featured non-lullaby songs as well.) Disney and Sesame Street/Muppet soundtracks and anthologies were excluded from the project because these companies: (1) frequently repackage their recordings, and (2) the songs are too closely identified with specific, popular characters to stand alone for purposes of this project. Several other wonderful recordings unfortunately did not make the final listing, not because of the quality of the music, but because the songs did not fit any of the subjects contained in the project. Taj Mahal's excellent *Shake Sugaree* is one such recording. Many other fine recordings had to be dropped from consideration because they are no longer available from distributors. And since this is a select list, many recordings considered were dropped because they couldn't compare in musical quality to the recordings in this book.

How to Use This Book

The selected songs fall into thirty-five subjects that are popular themes for story programs and classroom use. Song titles are listed alphabetically within each subject section. The titles are followed by the name of the artist and the name of the recording on which the song can be found. A brief annotation describes the song and usually includes programming ideas. These ideas vary from simple directions, felt board possibilities, prop ideas, or matching the songs with specific picture books. Some annotations simply call attention to special qualities of the song. Some annotations refer to similar songs. In cases where many recordings contain the same song, the version I find works best with an audience is usually the one listed at the beginning of the annotation. I also mention songwriters—when such information was available—in the annotations.

Suggested age levels can be found at the end of each annotation. "Ps" refers to Preschoolers (ages two through five), "Pr" refers to Primary Grades (ages six through eight), and "I" refers to Intermediate Grades (ages nine through twelve). All age designations are general suggestions and should be treated as such. There have been many exceptions when I have used preschool music on nine-year-olds with success. However, there have been many times when a song backfired because it wasn't age-appropriate for the audience.

Titles especially suited for adults with limited musical backgrounds have been identified with an asterisk (*). These songs are characterized by their simple, often repetitive patterns. Many of these songs can be recited if not sung.

At the end of each section, I list the title, performer, and recording of many additional songs that fit the section category.

A discography following this introduction lists all 308 recordings alphabetically by artist. Each artist listing contains the title of his or her recording, the production company, and publication date. A list of distributors who carry these titles can be found in the appendix. Because so many cassette recordings are being supplemented by CD-audios, we don't specify format in our listings. Check with distributors for the format of your choice.

For those interested in starting a core collection of children's recorded music, but are overwhelmed by the number of titles, a short listing of my favorite twenty children's musical recordings is provided with a brief description of each title.

In addition to the thirty-five subject listings with annotations, a section called "Short Takes" features another dozen topics that I do not personally use in my programs, but that other people might find useful for their particular needs. Many titles in these lists (and in the "format" lists described below) are not mentioned under the main subject listings and thus add to your program choices.

Don't overlook the section on song formats. Many of these songs are popular for programs regardless of their subject. This section lists call-and-response songs, cumulative songs, songs in foreign languages, rounds, and songs that feature sound effects. These terms are defined in this section. Other terms used throughout the book include "pattern songs" or "zipper songs," songs structured with a pattern that is repeated over and over, and "head hummers," tunes so catchy that you find yourself humming them in your head throughout the day.

Finally, I'd like to emphasize that this book alone does not bring programs to life. The book serves only as a guide. It is the recordings that are at the core of this project. You must listen to the recordings to put the ideas in this book to use. Buy, beg, or borrow the recordings featured in this work. Use your library's interlibrary loan services. Develop a resource-sharing network with other adults interested in children's recorded music. Do not make bootleg copies of the recordings, however. Many of the artists represented are truly dependent on the income from their recording sales.

Listen to the magic these artists have created. We are all lucky to have their talent preserved on tape and compact discs. May they continue to add more music to the worldwide children's jukebox.

Discography
of
Featured
Recordings

Abell, Timmy. The Farmer's Market. Upstream Records, 1989.

____. Play All Day. Upstream Records, 1992.

Alsop, Peter. Stayin' Over. Moose School Records, 1987.

____. Take Me with You. Moose School Records, 1986.

____. Wha'd'ya Wanna Do? Moose School Records, 1983.

American Children. Alacazam! 1989.

Arnold, Linda. Happiness Cake. A & M Records, 1989.

____. Make Believe. A & M Records, 1986.

____. Peppermint Wings. A & M Records, 1990.

____. The Rainbow Palace. A & M Records, 1991.

Atkinson, Lisa. I Wanna Tickle the Fish. A Gentle Wind, 1987.

____. The One and Only Me. A Gentle Wind, 1989.

Avni, Fran. Artichokes and Brussel Sprouts. Lemonstone Records, 1988.

____. Daisies and Ducklings. Lemonstone Records, 1990.

Banana Slug String Band. Adventures on the Air Cycle. Music for Little People, 1989.

____. Dirt Made My Lunch. Music for Little People, 1989.

____. Slugs at Sea. Music for Little People, 1991.

Baron, Laura, and Patti Dallas. Songs for the Earth. Golden Glow Recordings, 1992.

Bartels, Joanie. Bathtime Magic. Discovery Music, 1989.

_____. Jump for Joy. Discovery Music, 1993.

_____. Sillytime Magic. Discovery Music, 1989.

_____. Travelin' Magic. Discovery Music, 1988.

Bennett, Glenn. I Must Be Growing. ZOOM Express, 1992.

Berman, Marcia. Marcia Berman Sings Malvina Reynolds' Rabbits Dance. B/B Records, 1985.

Bethie. Bethie's Really Silly Songs about Animals. Discovery Music, 1993.

_____. Bethie's Really Silly Songs about Numbers. Discovery Music, 1993.

Bishop, Heather. Bellybutton. Mother of Pearl Records, 1982.

_____. Purple People Eater. Mother of Pearl Records, 1985.

Block, Cathy. Timeless. IMI Records, 1994.

Brown, Greg. Bathtub Blues. Red House Records, 1993.

Buchman, Rachel. Hello Everybody. A Gentle Wind, 1986.

_____. Hello Rachel! Hello Children! Rounder Records, 1988.

Buckner, Janice. All Aboard the Learn Along Train. Moonlight Rose, 1993.

_____. Everybody's Special. Moonlight Rose, 1993.

_____. Little Friends for Little Folks. A Gentle Wind, 1986.

The Bumblebeez. Animaland. Bumble Buzz Records, 1992.

Cappelli, Frank. Pass the Coconut. A & M Records, 1991.

_____. Take a Seat! A & M Records, 1993.

Carfra, Pat. Babes, Beasts, and Birds. Lullaby Lady Productions, 1987.

_____. Lullabies and Laughter with the Lullaby Lady Productions, 1982.

_____. Songs for Sleepyheads and Out-of-Beds. Lullaby Lady Productions, 1984.

Cassidy, Nancy. Kids' Songs. Klutz Press, 1986.

_____. Kids' Songs 2. Klutz Press, 1989.

_____. Kids' Songs Jubilee. Klutz Press, 1990.

_____. Kids' Songs Sleepyheads. Klutz Press, 1992.

Chapin, Tom. Billy the Squid. Sony , 1992.

____. Family Tree. Sony, 1988.

____. Moonboat. Sony, 1989.

____. Mother Earth. Sony, 1990.

____. Zag Zig. Sony, 1994.

Charette, Rick. Alligator in the Elevator. Pine Point Records, 1985.

____. Bubble Gum and Other Songs for Hungry Kids. Educational Activities, 1983.

____. Chickens on Vacation. Pine Point Records, 1990.

____. Where Do My Sneakers Go at Night? Pine Point Records, 1987.

The Chenille Sisters. 1-2-3 for Kids. Red House Records, 1989.

____. The Big Picture. Red House Records, 1992.

A Child's Celebration of Song. Music for Little People, 1992.

Colleen and Uncle Squaty. Colleen and Uncle Squaty. Hannafin/Woody, 1993.

Cowboy Steff. The Giving Tree and Other Shel Silverstein Songs. Sony, 1992.

Craig 'n Co. Morning 'n Night. Disney, 1992.

____. Rock 'n Together. Disney, 1992.

____. Rock 'n Toontown. Disney, 1993.

Crow, Dan. A Friend, a Laugh, a Walk in the Woods. Sony, 1992.

____. Oops! Rounder Records, 1988.

Dallas, Patti, and Laura Baron. Good Morning Sunshine. Golden Glow Recordings, 1986.

____. Playtime Parade. Golden Glow Recordings, 1989.

Diamond, Charlotte. 10 Carrot Diamond. Hug Bug Records, 1985.

____. Diamond in the Rough. Hug Bug Records, 1986.

____. Diamonds and Dragons. Hug Bug Records, 1988.

____. My Bear Gruff. Hug Bug Records, 1992.

Drake, David HB. Kid-Stuff. Makin' Jam, Etc. 1989.

Early Ears: Songs Just for 1 Year Olds. ZOOM Express, 1992.

Early Ears: Songs Just for 2 Year Olds. ZOOM Express, 1992.

Early Ears: Songs Just for 4 Year Olds. ZOOM Express, 1992.

Early Ears: Songs Just for 5 Year Olds. ZOOM Express, 1992.

Early Ears: Songs Just for 6 Year Olds. ZOOM Express, 1992.

Family Folk Festival. Music for Little People, 1990.

Feinstein, Michael. Pure Imagination. Elektra, 1992.

Fink, Cathy. Grandma Slid down the Mountain. Rounder Records, 1987.

____. When the Rain Comes Down. Rounder Records, 1987.

Fink, Cathy, and Marcy Marxer. A Cathy and Marcy Collection for Kids. Rounder Records, 1994.

____. Help Yourself. Rounder Records, 1990.

The Flyers. Family Hug. Flyertunes Hootentoot, 1989.

____. Your Smile. Flyertunes Hootentoot, 1991.

Foote, Norman. Foote Prints. Disney, 1991.

____. If the Shoe Fits. Disney, 1992.

Garcia, Jerry, and David Grissman. Not for Kids Only. Acoustic Disc, 1993.

Gemini. Good Mischief. Gemini, 1982.

____. Growing Up Together. Gemini, 1988.

____. Pulling Together. Gemini Records, n.d.

Gibson, Dee, and Joe Scruggs. Songs to Brighten Your Day. Educational Graphics Press, 1984.

Grammer, Red. Can You Sound Just like Me? Smilin' Atcha Music, 1983.

____. Down the Do-Re-Mi. Smilin' Atcha Music, 1991.

____. Red Grammer's Favorite Sing Along Songs. Smilin' Atcha Music, 1993.

____. Teaching Peace. Smilin' Atcha Music, 1986.

Grandma's Patchwork Quilt. American Melody, 1987.

The Green Chili Jam Band. Starfishing. Green Chili Jam, 1993.

Greg and Steve. Kidding Around. Youngheart Records, 1985.

____. Kids in Motion. Youngheart Records, 1987.

____. On the Move. Youngheart Records, 1983.

____. Playing Favorites. Youngheart Records, 1991.

____. We All Live Together, Vol. 1. Youngheart Records, 1975.

____. We All Live Together, Vol. 2. Youngheart Records, 1978.

____. We All Live Together, Vol. 3. Youngheart Records, 1979.

____. We All Live Together, Vol. 4. Youngheart Records, 1980.

____. We All Live Together, Vol. 5. Youngheart Records, 1994.

Grunsky, Jack. Children of the Morning. Youngheart Records, 1992.

____. Waves of Wonder. Youngheart Records, 1992.

Guthrie, Woody. Woody's 20 Grow Big Songs. Warner Brothers, 1992.

Harley, Bill. 50 Ways to Fool Your Mother. Round River Records, 1986.

____. Big Big World. A & M Records, 1993.

____. Monsters in the Bathroom. Round River Records, 1984.

____. You're in Trouble. Round River Records, 1988.

Herdman, Priscilla. Daydreamer. Music for Little People, 1993.

____. Stardreamer. Music for Little People, 1988.

Ives, Burl. The Best of Burl's for Boys and Girls. MCA Records, 1980.

____. The Little White Duck. MCA Records, 1974.

Janet and Judy. Good Clean Fun. Janet and Judy Records, 1990.

____. Hotbilly Hits. Janet and Judy Records, 1993.

____. Musical Almanac. Janet and Judy Records, 1986.

Jenkins, Ella. I Know the Colors of the Rainbow. Educational Activities, 1981.

____. You'll Sing a Song and I'll Sing a Song. Smithsonian/Folkways, 1989.

Jennings, Waylon. Cowboys, Sisters, Rascals, and Dirt. Ode 2 Kids, 1993.

Kahn, Si. Good Times and Bed Times. Rounder Records, 1993.

Kaye, Danny. Danny Kaye for Children. MCA Records, 1959.

Kinnoin, Dave. Daring Dewey. Song Wizard Records, 1990.

____. Dunce Cap Kelly. Song Wizard Records, 1993.

____. Fun-a-Rooey. Song Wizard Records, 1987.

LaFond, Lois. I Am Who I Am! ZOOM Express, 1992.

____. One World. Lois LaFond, 1990.

Lewis, Shari. Lamb Chop's Sing-Along, Play-Along. A & M
    Records, 1988.

Little Richard. Shake It All About. Disney, 1992.

Livingston, Bob. Open the Window. A Gentle Wind, 1991.

Lonnquist, Ken. A Little Dreamin'. Maple Twig Music, 1986.

____. Welcome 2 Kenland. Maple Twig Music, 1992.

Marin, Cheech. My Name Is Cheech, the School Bus Driver.
    Rincon, 1992.

Marxer, Marcy. Jump Children. Rounder Records, 1986.

McCornack, Mike and Carleen. Beasties, Bumbershoots, and
    Lullabies. Alacazam! 1992.

____. Sunshine Cake. Alacazam! 1993.

McCutcheon, John. Family Garden. Rounder Records, 1993.

____. Howjadoo. Rounder Records, 1987.

____. Mail Myself to You. Rounder Records, 1988.

Miché, Mary. Animal Crackers. Song Trek Music, 1988.

____. Earthy Tunes. Song Trek Music, 1987.

____. Kid's Stuff. Song Trek Music, 1986.

____. Nature Nuts. Song Trek Music, 1990.

____. Peace It Together. Song Trek Music, 1989.

Mish, Michael. A Kid's Eye View of the Environment. Mish
    Mash Music, 1989.

Monet, Lisa. Circle Time. Music for Little People, 1986.

____. Jump Down. Music for Little People, 1987.

____. My Best Friend. Music for Little People, 1991.

Muldaur, Maria. On the Sunny Side. Music for Little People,
    1990.

Nagler, Eric. Come On In. Elephant Records, 1985.

____. Fiddle Up a Tune. Elephant Records, 1982.

____. Improvise with Eric Nagler. Rounder Records, 1989.

Neat, Roxanne, and David Stoeri. The Bell Cow Swing. Hot
    Coffee, 1993.

____. Dance, Boatman, Dance. Neat & Stoeri, 1988.

____. Hummin' Words. Neat & Stoeri, 1987.

Noah, Tim. In Search of the Wow Wow Wibble Woggle Wazzie
    Woodle Woo! Noazart, 1983.

O'Brien, Bruce. In My Family's House. Song Circle Productions, 1989.

Palmer, Hap. Babysong. Educational Activity Records, 1984.

____. Can a Cherry Pie Wave Goodbye? Hap-Pal Music, 1991.

____. More Baby Songs. Educational Activity Records, 1981.

____. Peek-a-Boo. Hap-Pal Music, 1990.

Parachute Express. Circle of Friends. Disney, 1991.

____. Feel the Music. Disney, 1991.

____. Happy to Be Here. Disney, 1991.

____. Over Easy. Disney, 1992.

____. Shakin' It! Disney, 1992.

____. Sunny Side Up. Disney, 1991.

Paxton, Tom. Balloon-Alloon-Alloon. PAX Records, 1987.

____. The Marvellous Toy. PAX Records, 1984, 1991.

____. Peanut Butter Pie. Sony, 1990.

____. Suzy Is a Rocker. Sony, 1992.

Peace Is the World Smiling. Music for Little People, 1989.

Peanutbutterjam. Incredibly Spreadable. Peanutbutterjam, 1984.

____. Peanutbutterjam Goes to School. Peanutbutterjam, 1986.

____. Simply Singable. Peanutbutterjam, 1988.

Pease, Tom. Boogie Boogie Boogie. Tomorrow River Music, 1985.

____. I'm Gonna Reach. Tomorrow River Music, 1989.

____. Wobbi-Do-Wop. Tomorrow River Music, 1993.

Pelham, Ruth. Under One Sky. A Gentle Wind, 1982.

Penner, Fred. The Cat Came Back. Oak Street Music, 1980.

____. Collections. Oak Street Music, 1989.

____. Ebeneezer Sneezer. Oak Street Music, 1991.

____. Fred Penner's Place. Oak Street Music, 1988.

____. Happy Feet. Oak Street Music, 1992.

____. A House for Me. Oak Street Music, 1985.

____. Poco. Oak Street Music, 1991.

____. What a Day! Oak Street Music, 1994.

Peter, Paul and Mary. Peter, Paul and Mommy. Warner Brothers, 1969.

____. Peter, Paul and Mommy, Too. Warner Brothers, 1993.

Phipps, Bonnie. Dinosaur Choir. Wimmer-Ferguson, 1992.

____. Monsters' Holiday. Wimmer-Ferguson, 1994.

Pirtle, Sarah. Magical Earth. A Gentle Wind, 1993.

____. Two Hands Hold the Earth. A Gentle Wind, 1984.

____. The Wind Is Telling Secrets. A Gentle Wind, 1988.

Polisar, Barry Louis. Family Concert. Rainbow Morning Music, 1990.

____. Family Trip. Rainbow Morning Music, 1993.

____. Old Dog, New Tricks. Rainbow Morning Music, 1993.

____. Teacher's Favorites. Rainbow Morning Music, 1993.

Put on Your Green Shoes. Sony, 1993.

Quackity Yakity Bop. Music for Little People, 1988.

Raffi. Baby Beluga. MCA Records, 1977.

____. Corner Grocery Store. MCA Records, 1979.

____. Evergreen, Everblue. MCA Records, 1990.

____. Everything Grows. MCA Records, 1987.

____. More Singable Songs. MCA Records, 1977.

____. One Light, One Sun. MCA Records, 1985.

____. Raffi in Concert with the Rise and Shine Band. MCA Records, 1989.

____. Raffi on Broadway. MCA Records, 1993.

____. Rise and Shine. MCA Records, 1982.

____. Singable Songs for the Very Young. MCA Records, 1976.

Rainbow Sign. Rounder Records, 1992.

Rappin' Rob. The Rappin' Rob Rap. The Kid-Tested Company, 1992.

Reggae for Kids. RAS Records, 1992.

Rockow, Corrine. I Sing Every Day of My Life. Tomorrow River Music, 1991.

Rogers, Sally. Piggyback Planet. Round River Records, 1990.

____. What Can One Little Person Do? Round River Records, 1992.

Rory. I'm Just a Kid. Roar Music, 1987.

____. Make-Believe Day. Sony, 1989.

Rosen, Gary. Tot Rock. Lightyear, 1993.

Rosenshontz. Family Vacation. Lightyear, 1988.

____. It's the Truth. Lightyear, 1984.

____. Rock 'n' Roll Teddy Bear. Lightyear, 1986.

____. Rosenshontz Tickles You. Lightyear, 1980.

____. Share It. Lightyear, 1982.

____. Uh-Oh. Lightyear, 1990.

Rosenthal, Phil. Chickens in the Garden. American Melody, 1990.

____. Comin' round the Mountain. American Melody, 1993.

____. The Paw Paw Patch. American Melody, 1987.

Roth, Kevin. Daddysongs. Sony, 1992.

____. Dinosaurs, Dragons, and Other Children's Songs. Marlboro Records, 1990.

____. Oscar, Bingo, and Buddies. Marlboro Records, 1990.

____. The Sandman. Marlboro Records, 1988.

____. The Secret Journey. Marlboro Records, 1987.

____. Travel Song Sing Alongs. Marlboro Records, 1994.

____. Unbearable Bears. Marlboro Records, 1986.

Schneider, Bob. Listen to the Children. Compose, 1989.

____. When You Dream a Dream. Peter Pan, 1987.

Scooter. Calling All Kids. Jimmy Jangle Records, 1992.

____. Miles of Smiles. Jimmy Jangle Records, 1992.

Scruggs, Joe. Abracadabra. Educational Graphics Press, 1986.

____. Ants. Educational Graphics Press, 1994.

____. Bahamas Pajamas. Educational Graphics Press, 1990.

____. Deep in the Jungle. Educational Graphics Press, 1987.

____. Even Trolls Have Moms. Educational Graphics Press, 1988.

____. Late Last Night. Educational Graphics Press, 1984.

____. Traffic Jams. Educational Graphics Press, 1985.

Seeger, Mike and Peggy. American Folk Songs for Children. Rounder Records, 1987.

Seeger, Pete. Abiyoyo and Other Story Songs for Children. Smithsonian/Folkways, 1989.

____. Family Concert. Sony, 1992.

____. Stories and Songs for Little Children. High Windy Audio, n.d.

The Seeger Family. Animal Folk Songs for Children. Rounder Records, 1992.

Shake It to the One That You Love the Best. Warren-Mattox Productions, 1989.

Sharon, Lois and Bram. All the Fun You Can Sing! Elephant Records, 1993.

____. The Elephant Show Record. Elephant Records, 1986.

____. Great Big Hits. Elephant Records, 1992.

____. Happy Birthday. Elephant Records, 1988.

____. In the Schoolyard. Elephant Records, 1980.

____. Mainly Mother Goose. Elephant Records, 1984.

____. One Elephant, Deux Elephants. Elephant Records, 1980.

____. One, Two, Three, Four, Live! Elephant Records, 1982.

____. Sing A to Z. Elephant Records, 1990.

____. Singing 'n Swinging. Elephant Records, 1980.

____. Smorgasbord. Elephant Records, 1980.

____. Stay Tuned. Elephant Records, 1987.

Shontz, Bill. Animal Tales. Lightyear, 1993.

Silverstein, Shel. Where the Sidewalk Ends. Columbia, 1984.

The Singing Rainbow Youth Ensemble. Head First and Belly Down. Sisters' Choice Recordings, 1992.

Sprout, Jonathan. On the Radio. Sprout Records, 1986.

Staines, Bill. The Happy Wanderer. Red House Records, 1993.

Sweet Honey in the Rock. All for Freedom. Tickle Tune Typhoon, 1989.

____. I Got Shoes. Music for Little People, 1994.

Tickle Tune Typhoon. All of Us Will Shine. Tickle Toon Typhoon, 1987.

____. Circle Around. Tickle Tune Typhoon, 1983.

____. Healthy Beginnings. Music for Little People, 1993.

____. Hearts and Hands. Tickle Tune Typhoon, 1991.

____. Hug the Earth. Tickle Tune Typhoon, 1985.

Tracey, Paul. The Rainbow Kingdom. A Gentle Wind, 1985.

Troubadour. Are We Almost There? A Gentle Wind, 1984.

____. Can We Go Now? A Gentle Wind, 1987.

____. On the Trail. A Gentle Wind, 1990.

Trout Fishing in America. Big Trouble. Trout Records, 1991.

Ungar, Jay, and Lyn Hardy. A Place to Be. A Gentle Wind, 1981.

The Van Manens. Healthy Planet, Healthy People. People Records, 1994.

____. We Recycle. People Records, 1990.

Van Ronk, Dave. Peter and the Wolf. Alacazam! 1990.

Vitamin L. Everyone's Invited. Loveable Creature Music, 1991.

____. Singin' in the Key of L. Loveable Creature Music, 1992.

____. Walk a Mile. Loveable Creature Music, 1989.

Walker, Mary Lu. The Frog's Party. A Gentle Wind, 1989.

Watson, Doc. Doc Watson Sings Songs for Little Pickers. Alacazam! 1990.

Wee Sing. Price Stern Sloan, 1977.

Wee Sing and Play. Price Stern Sloan, 1986.

Wee Sing around the World. Price Stern Sloan, 1994.

Wee Sing Fun 'n' Folk. Price Stern Sloan, 1989.

Wee Sing Silly Songs. Price Stern Sloan, 1986.

Wee Sing Sing-Alongs. Price Stern Sloan, 1982.

Weissman, Jackie. Peanut Butter, Tarzan, and Roosters. Jackie Weissman, 1981.

Wellington, Bill. WOOF Hits Home. Well-In-Tune Productions, 1991.

____. WOOF Hits the Road. Well-In-Tune Productions, 1992.

____. WOOF's Greatest Bits. Well-In-Tune Productions, 1993.

Whiteley, Ken. All of the Seasons. Alacazam! 1993.

Winter, Cathy, and Betsy Rose. As Strong As Anyone Can Be. A Gentle Wind, 1982.

Wozniak, Doug. Hugs and Kisses. Come Alive, 1994.

____. Music for Miles of Smiles. Come Alive, 1991.

The Robbie Award
Hall of Fame

The Top Twenty Children's Musical Recordings

Choosing your starter or core collection from the 300 recordings listed in this book can be overwhelming. That's why the Robbie Awards for the Best Children's Musical Recordings were created. The Robbie Awards are given annually by myself (usually just for myself and my library customers) to sort out the nuggets of gold from the dozens of new titles available. Listed below are twenty of my all-time favorites. You may want to consider starting a collection from this list for your school, library, or home. Here then, listed alphabetically by artist, is the all-time Robbie Award Hall of Fame.

1. Brown, Greg. Bathtub Blues.

This popular folk musician scores big with his first children's recording. The gruff singing voice contrasted with the gentle, nostalgic, and often humorous childhood topics makes for an appealing work of art. "Late Night Radio" details long nighttime rides in the back seat of the family car with the radio picking up music from far away states. "I Remember When" is a sweet reminder to parents not to be too tough on their children when they are naughty (especially if a grandmother is around to remind everyone how the parent acted when he or she was a child). Other highlights include "Young Robin," a song about learning to fly; "Flabbergabble" ("I'm gonna skibblejibble gabbaflabba wungamunga you"); a gritty version of "Shake Sugaree"; the lovely "You Might as Well Go to Sleep"; and the title song.

2. Buchman, Rachel. Hello Everybody.

This Rachel Buchman tape is my favorite source of songs to use for our Tales for Twos toddler program. Buchman has a natural way with young children, gently leading them to be creative without talking down to them or bouncing around the room to get their attention. Her versions of "I Had a Rooster," "Five Little Ducks," and "Little Red Wagon" are the best ways of introducing traditional folk songs to the very young. When my son Sam was three, we always sang Buchman's "I Think I'll Try Some" as we went for walks or rides in the car. Be sure to try "Hello Everybody" on your young children.

3. Chapin, Tom. Billy the Squid.

How do I choose one Tom Chapin recording over another? It's nearly impossible. Chapin and his songwriting partner John Forster are two of the most creative children's songwriters today. They inject creative wordplay, story lines, and musical arrangements in all of their songs, no matter what topic. *Billy the Squid* is the recording I keep coming back to when I need to be reminded of how great minds work. There is not one ordinary song in the bunch; they are all wonderful. "Bye Bye Dodo," "Great Big Words," "All of My Friends," "Happy Earth Day," "Preacher Herman," "The Missing Parade"—I'm humming them as I type this! And my absolute favorite Chapin song, "Bedtime Round," helps bring the recording to an end.

4. Diamond, Charlotte. 10 Carrot Diamond.

This Juno Award winner is Diamond's first and best recording. Starting with the catchy "Four Hugs a Day" all the way through to "10 Crunchy Carrots," this recording is a fun-filled adventure. Diamond covers several children's modern classics such as "I Am a Pizza," "I Wanna Be a Dog," and "May There Always Be Sunshine," as well as her originals "Sasquatch," "Looking for Dracula," and my favorite Diamond song, "Spider's Web."

5. Fink, Cathy, and Marcy Marxer. A Cathy and Marcy Collection for Kids.

These two artists have some of the best solo recordings for children ever made. I'm copping out by including their greatest hits package, just to keep my list to twenty recordings. You should really purchase Fink's *Grandma Slid down the Mountain* and *When the Rain Comes Down,* and Marxer's *Jump Children.* But for economy's sake, you'll do almost as well with this wonderful collection. "Susie and the Alligator," "It's a Beautiful Day," "When the Rain Comes Down," and "Jump Children" are my personal favorites out of the seventeen songs included in this package.

6. Grammer, Red. Down the Do-Re-Mi.

This guy can sing! Some of Grammer's other recordings may be more popular, but this is the recording that showcases his strength as a songwriter. With his partner Kathy Grammer, they have created some beautiful songs that will one day be recognized as some of the best from this era. "The ABC's of You," "Heading On Down to the Barn," "Two Hands Four Hands," "Brothers and Sisters," and the title song are the strongest originals from this set. Grammer also does a marvelous job of covering traditional songs and other people's works, including "Place in the Choir," "Land of the Silver Birch," "Rattlin' Bog," and "Grandfather's Clock."

7. Guthrie, Woody. Woody's 20 Grow Big Songs.

The Guthrie family recently recorded several of the late Woody Guthrie's children's songs. Some songs are actually old recordings of Woody singing by himself. Others are newly recorded by Arlo Guthrie and other members of the Guthrie family. And on a few songs, the family mixed old recordings of

Woody with the new recordings. It's as if he was trading verses with the modern-day singers. On the beautiful "Needle Sing," Woody trades lines with Arlo while the youngest generation sings in the background. Guthrie was a master of wordplay as shown in the songs "Cleano," "Mailman," "Bling Blang," "Riding in My Car," "Pretty and Shinyo," and "Howdy Doo." He could also write a pretty melody such as "My Dolly" and "Sleep Eye." These songs have been staples for years and will remain timeless.

8. Herdman, Priscilla. Daydreamer.

Herdman delivers crystal-clear interpretations of modern-day children's classics. John Gorka's "Branching Out," John McCutcheon's "Kindergarten Wall" and "Water from Another Time," Bob Devlin's "When the Rain Comes Down," Carol Johnson's "Love Grows One by One," and Bill Harley's "Where Have You Been" are just a few. Herdman also added music to the text of two children's picture books, *A Fairy Went A-Marketing* and *Hard Scrabble Harvest.* Put this recording on and get lost in it.

9. McCutcheon, John. Howjadoo.

When I'm in the mood for dulcimers, fiddles, and banjos, I put on John McCutcheon. Special treatment is given to the lively "Cut the Cake," "Howjadoo," "Rubber Blubber Whale," and "All God's Critters." There are touching renditions of "Here's to Cheshire" and "Tender Shepherd." Plus, the hilarious "Peanut Butter," a story told by guest storyteller Barbara Freeman of the Folktellers. McCutcheon's other children's recordings *Mail Myself to You* and *Family Garden* are so good, they too make this a tough choice.

10. Nagler, Eric. Improvise with Eric Nagler.

If I was forced at gunpoint to name one children's musical recording over all the rest, I would probably choose this Nagler masterpiece. Nagler put all of his talent into this project and created a touchstone for all other children's performers. The recording starts out with a wonderful rendition of Woody Guthrie's "Howjadoo" and ends with the quiet "Lula Lullaby." In between is a combination of beautiful melodies, hard-driving rock 'n' roll, fall-down-on-the-floor humor, touching emotions, cacaphony, and chaos. My personal favorites include Nagler's new interpretation of "Mairzy Doats"; the originals "Just Not Fair," "The Body Song," "Super Mom," and "You Just Improvise"; a haunting version of "Cluck Old Hen"; the nostalgic "Jumping in the Leaves"; and the hilarious "Dueling Tubas." This recording requires several listenings to catch all of the background goings-on with bells, whistles, spoons, harps, and something called a sewerphone accenting the songs. Check it out.

11. Pease, Tom. Boogie Boogie Boogie.

I don't know of a more energetic person in the children's music industry than Tom Pease. He has more energy left after an hour show than most of us have the whole day. And that energy carries over to his recordings. *I'm Gonna Reach* and *Wobbi-Do-Wop* are wonderful recordings, but I'm partial to *Boogie Boogie Boogie*. Highlights include "Swinging on a Star," "I'm a Little Cookie," "Many Cows," "What Does Your Mama Do," the outstanding "World Citizen," and the beautiful closer "Sabunana Kusasa." There is a lot of both silliness and seriousness on this whirlwind tape.

12. Pelham, Ruth. Under One Sky.

Pelham is one of those rare songwriters who can tap directly into a child's emotions and self-esteem. Her title song is already a classic in children's musical circles. "If I Could Be Anything" and "Rainbow 'round Me" are my two favorites. Pelham explores the creative side of children as demonstrated by "Shaker Song," "Guitar Box Band," and "If I Could Be Anyone." "Wake You in the Morning" and "I Cried" are very comforting songs. I hope we don't have too long a wait for the next Ruth Pelham children's recording.

13. Peter, Paul and Mary. Peter, Paul and Mommy, Too.

The public had to wait more than twenty years between the first sensational Peter, Paul and Mommy recording and this one.

To say it was worth the wait is an understatement. The trio recorded this live before a New York audience. Peter, Paul and Mary perform gorgeous renditions of "Garden Song," and "Somos el barco." They have a hilarious interpretation of "I Know an Old Lady Who Swallowed a Fly" complete with an Elvis impersonation. And, of course, everyone in the audience knows all of the words to their classic "Puff (The Magic Dragon)."

14. Pirtle, Sarah. Magical Earth.

A Gentle Wind is a children's recording company that has a very strong roster of performers. My favorite is Sarah Pirtle who has three children's recordings: *Two Hands Hold the Earth, The Wind Is Telling Secrets,* and *Magical Earth.* Pirtle is a strong song-writer who specializes in beautiful melodies and excellent arrangements. *Magical Earth* contains a variety of American folk, zydeco, Caribbean, and Latin American styles. My favorites from this recording include "The Other Side of the World," "Paz y libertad," "Walls and Bridges," "Follow the Voice," and "Magical Earth." All in all, a fine showcase of our global music community.

15. Polisar, Barry Louis. Old Dog, New Tricks.

Polisar carried out a very smart marketing idea by taking his best songs from a twenty-year career, re-recording them with top-notch musicians, and then re-packaging them by themes. *Family Trip* features his best family songs and *Teacher's Favorites* contains his best school songs. *Old Dog, New Tricks* has some of my favorite Polisar songs, his animal songs. Many musicians have recorded his popular "I Wanna Be a Dog" and "I'm a 3-Toed, Triple-Eyed, Double-Jointed Dinosaur." Other highlights include "Our Dog Bernard," "The Skatter Brak Flath Who Lives in My Bath," and "I've Got a Dog and My Dog's Name Is Cat." There are some non-animal treasures such as "The Apple of My Eye" and "Giggle Tickle Fiddle Little Wiggle Around." I hope other children's performers follow Polisar's example and fine-tune some of their past work in packages such as this.

16. Raffi. Singable Songs for the Very Young.

17. Raffi. More Singable Songs.

Raffi is probably the most popular children's musical performer ever, selling zillions of copies of *Baby Beluga, Rise and Shine, Evergreen Everblue,* and other wonderful recordings. But I still think his best work can be found in his first two recordings, the Singable Songs series. From "The More We Get Together" to "New River Train," these recordings contain thirty-two of the best children's songs. I can sing several of these in storytime over and over without getting tired of them. "Spider on the Floor," "Down by the Bay," "Willoughby Wallaby Woo," "You Gotta Sing," "Mr. Sun," and "Shake My Sillies Out" are staples at our library. Both recordings are available on one compact disc, *The Raffi Singable Songs Collection* (A & M, 1988).

18. Rosenshontz. Share It.

Along with Raffi and Sharon, Lois and Bram, the duo Rosenshontz helped raise the popularity of children's music to new heights in the 1980s. *Share It* is one of their more solid efforts with songs such as "Happy Place," "Sleep Sleep," "Garbage," "Gonna Have a Good Time," and the title song. "Sounds from A to Z" is one of those songs that make you wonder how they ever thought of such a great idea. Gary Rosen and Bill Shontz are currently releasing solo albums, but like the Beatles, the real magic comes when they work together.

19. Sharon, Lois and Bram. Great Big Hits.

Thank goodness this greatest hits package came out in time for this Top Twenty list. I can again cop out and list one Sharon, Lois and Bram recording when this list should really include *Smorgasbord, Stay Tuned,* and *Mainly Mother Goose. Great Big Hits* is a wonderful bargain, though. It has more than thirty fun songs, including their two signature pieces, "One Elephant" and "Skinnamarink." Other favorites include "Little Rabbit Foo-Foo," "How Much Is That Doggie in the Window," "Rags," "Candy Man, Salty Dog," and "The Eensy Weensy Spider."

Sharon, Lois and Bram are at their best when taking familiar songs and creating the most marvelous arrangements possible.

20. I'm still trying to decide whether or not to put Mike and Carleen McCornack's *Beasties, Bumbershoots, and Lullabies* at number twenty, or Green Chili Jam Band's *Starfishing,* or *Circle of Friends* by Parachute Express, or *Big Big World* by Bill Harley, or *Doc Watson Sings Songs for Little Pickers,* or more Chapin, more Pirtle, more Polisar, more Herdman, more Fink, more Marxer, more McCutcheon, more Pease, more Raffi, or. . . . OK, it's a tough choice. It's an impossible choice. Make it your choice and start listening to the wonderful world of children's musical recordings. I know you'll soon be as big a fan as I am. Create your own core collection and let me know what you chose.

Happy listening.

Hello Songs

Establish a classroom or storytime routine by starting each session with a song of greeting.

"Come On In." Nagler, Eric. Come On In.

> Nagler sings "Come on in, ain't nobody here but me" in deep, falsetto, angry, and sexy tones. Have the children think of new ways to sing the phrase, such as blurbling their lips, crying, or laughing their way through it. Nagler winds the song down by singing it quieter and quieter until the children are silently mouthing the words. One final, loud "Come on in . . ." ends the song with a bang. *(All)*

"Hello." Arnold, Linda. Peppermint Wings.

> Arnold's call-and-response song features greetings in French, Spanish, Swedish, Hebrew, German, Japanese, Chinese, Italian, Russian, Hindu, Yugoslavian, and more. Several other songs that feature greetings in foreign languages include:

Key: Ps: Preschool, 2–5; Pr: Primary, 6–8; I: Intermediate, 9–12;
*: Simple tunes

"H-E-Double-L-O." Janet and Judy. Hotbilly Hits.

"Hello." Gemini. Growing Up Together.

"Hello! Hola!" Buckner, Janice. All Aboard the Learn Along Train.

"The Hello Song." (Fred Miller) Early Ears: Songs Just for 2 Year Olds.

"Hello to All the Children of the World." Wee Sing around the World.

"One Big Family." Schneider, Bob. Listen to the Children.

"Siyanibingelela." Grunsky, Jack. Waves of Wonder.   *(All)*

* "Hello." Weissman, Jackie. Peanut Butter, Tarzan, and Roosters.

Ella Jenkins wrote this very popular hello song. Weissman made it very funny by turning it into a body song complete with waving hands, flapping elbows, moving pinkie fingers (in pinkie finger voices), shaking heads, and flapping tongues.   *(Ps, Pr)*

* "Hello, Everybody." Buchman, Rachel. Hello Everybody.

Buchman sings hello to everybody and everything in the room including her guitar, fingers, mommy, and daddy. Have the children sing hello to other objects in the room (puppets, books, light switches). The book *Goodnight Moon* by Margaret Wise Brown is a nice contrast to the song. In the book, the reader says "goodnight" to several objects. "Hello, Everybody" was written by Charity Bailey.   *(Ps)*

* "Hello, Hello." Pelham, Ruth. Under One Sky.

Pelham's very simple, very short song makes a very effective program opening. Try it. You'll have it memorized in thirty seconds.   *(Ps)*

"Howdy Doo." Guthrie, Woody. Woody's 20 Grow Big Songs.

Woody Guthrie's exuberant song is possibly the most well-known hello song in musical circles. There are plenty of

Guthrie's playful lyrics present, including "How-ji-hee-ji-hi-ji-ho-ji." The song can also be found as "Howjadoo" on:
>   McCutcheon, John. Howjadoo.
>   Nagler, Eric. Improvise with Eric Nagler.   *(All)*

Here are more great hello songs:

"Everyone's Invited." Vitamin L. Everyone's Invited.

"How Do You Do?" Block, Cathy. Timeless.

"Howdy Neighbor." Monet, Lisa. My Best Friend.

"I Know Your Face." Pelham, Ruth. Under One Sky.

"Say Hello." Greg and Steve. Kidding Around.

"Say Hi." Grammer, Red. Teaching Peace.

"Shakin' Hands." Fink, Cathy. When the Rain Comes Down.

"Shakin' Hands." Fink, Cathy, and Marcy Marxer. A Cathy and Marcy Collection for Kids.

The Subject Listings

Anatomy

"Beanbag Boogie." Greg and Steve. Kids in Motion.

Children can dance to a funky beat with beanbags balanced on their heads, tummies, shoulders, elbows, and other parts of their bodies. If there aren't enough beanbags for the whole group, take turns (the song is long) or substitute tissue or felt squares. While the tissue and felt are not as challenging as the beanbags to balance, they will produce the same amount of giggles. Another beanbags-on-the-body song is Hap Palmer's "Bean Bag Alphabet Rag" from *Can a Cherry Pie Wave Goodbye?* **(Ps, Pr)**

"Bellybutton." Pease, Tom. I'm Gonna Reach.

Here is an ode to bellybuttons written by noted children's singwriter Connie ("If You Love a Hippopotamus") Kaldor. Any song that encourages kids to sing the word "bellybut-

---

Key: Ps: Preschool, 2–5; Pr: Primary, 6–8; I: Intermediate, 9–12;
    *: Simple tunes

ton" dozens of times has to be good. Play the recording and enjoy Pease's energetic presentation. "Bellybutton" can also be found on:

Bishop, Heather. Bellybutton. *(All)*

"The Body Song." Nagler, Eric. Improvise with Eric Nagler.

Nagler wrote this pun-filled song with Diana Buckley. There are several questions concerning riding on the bridge of one's nose, beating an ear drum, and using a key for the lock of one's hair. Nagler ends the song with a warning that he just might ask tougher questions than the ones he has been asked. This song is a special highlight of one of the best children's recordings ever produced. *(I)*

* "Nobody Else like Me." Walker, Mary Lu. The Frog's Party.

Walker's original cumulative song celebrates uniqueness (this is my hand, arm, leg, and more). Children can add their own verses. *(Ps)*

"One Little Nose." Bethie. Bethie's Really Silly Songs about Numbers.

Bethie wonders why we have two ears, ten toes, and lots of hair, but only one nose. She does, however, love the things her nose smells (popcorn, honeysuckle, and apple pie). Play the recording and have the kids touch their various body parts as Bethie sings about them. "One Little Nose" was written by Connie Kaldor. *(Ps, Pr)*

* "Put Your Finger in the Air." Guthrie, Woody. Woody's 20 Grow Big Songs.

Woody Guthrie wrote this, the classic body song. Put your finger in the air, on your head, nose, shoe, and chin. Ask the kids to help with new verses. "Put Your Finger in the Air" can also be found on:

Greg and Steve. Playing Favorites. *(Ps)*

* **"Put Your Finger On." Parachute Express. Feel the Music.**

We have lots of fun singing this simple tune during our library's Family Storytime. The kids stand up and put their fingers on their tummies, nose, ears, and whatever else they can suggest. After each section of the song, they turn around and clap. I have the grown-ups stand up for the last verse "now that they have had time to see how it is properly done." **(Ps, Pr)**

"Simon Says." Greg and Steve. We All Live Together, Vol. 3.

The regular "Simon Says" game is a challenge for both the leader and the followers. Greg and Steve have developed an easier version for young children, with no winners or losers. Listen to the recording as "Simon" directs the kids to touch their elbows, hair, ears, and more. **(Ps)**

* **"Tony Chestnut." Rappin' Rob. The Rappin' Rob Rap.**

"Tony Chestnut" is a popular, traditional camp favorite that is performed in several variations. Rappin' Rob includes two versions on his tape. Here are the words and motions to the first version. The children point to various body parts that are hidden in the name Tony Chestnut. "Tony Chestnut knows I love you, that's what Tony knows."

To-	(Point to your toe.)
-ny	(Point to your knee.)
Chest-	(Point to your chest.)
-nut	(Point to your head.)
knows	(Point to your nose.)
I	(Point to your eye.)
love	(Point to your heart.)
you	(Point to your friend.)
that's what	(Clap twice.) **(Ps, Pr)**

"Two Hands Four Hands." Grammer, Red. Down the Do-Re-Mi.

This is an energetic, loud, and challenging call-and-response song. Grammer sings about using hands for work.

Parents will find this an inspirational exercise for the kids to perform before sending them off to do chores. Play the recording and let the kids respond to Grammer's rap. But if you want their mouths to drop open in astonishment, memorize the army drill-like cadence yourself. "Two Hands Four Hands" was written by Red and Kathy Grammer.

(Pr, I)

* **"Where Is Thumbkin?" Wee Sing.**

This traditional fingerplay song is for the youngest child. Wee Sing's version goes through all five fingers and their nicknames (Pointer, Tall Man, Ring Man, Baby, and All the Men). The accompanying booklet suggests applying the tune to hands and feet as well. "Where Is Thumbkin?" can also be found on:

Dallas, Patti, and Laura Baron. Playtime Parade.
Sharon, Lois and Bram. In the Schoolyard.

A similar song is "Tommy Thumb" on Sharon, Lois and Bram's *Stay Tuned*. This song features lots of movement ("dance him on your shoulder," "dance him on your knee") with Tommy Thumb, Peter Pointer, Toby Tall, Ruby Ring, and Baby Finger, who make up the Finger Family. "Tommy Thumb" can also be found on:

Colleen and Uncle Squaty. Colleen and Uncle Squaty.

(Ps)

"Wiggle in My Toe." Scruggs, Joe. Late Last Night.

The kids will find wiggles in their toes, feet, knees, seats, tummies, arms, hands, heads, and hair in this cumulative song. Scruggs wants the wiggles to stop because they make him giggle. Play the recording and wiggle away. "Wiggle in My Toe" was written by Joe and Linda Scruggs. *(Ps,Pr)*

Here are more great songs about anatomy:

"The Apple of My Eye." Polisar, Barry Louis. Old Dog, New Tricks.

"Belly Button." Scruggs, Joe. Late Last Night.

"Body Machine." Buckner, Janice. All Aboard the Learning Train.

"The Body Rock." Greg and Steve. Kidding Around.

"The Body Rock." Greg and Steve. Kids in Motion.

"The Body Song." Lewis, Shari. Lamb Chop's Sing-Along, Play-Along.

"Do Your Ears Hang Low?" Bartels, Joanie. Sillytime Magic.

"Do Your Ears Hang Low?" Cassidy, Nancy. Kids' Songs Jubilee.

"Do Your Ears Hang Low?" Roth, Kevin. Oscar, Bingo, and Buddies.

"Do Your Ears Hang Low?" Sharon, Lois and Bram. Stay Tuned.

"Do Your Ears Hang Low?" Wee Sing Silly Songs.

"Doctor Knickerbocker." Sharon, Lois and Bram. All the Fun You Can Sing!

"Doctor Knickerbocker." Sharon, Lois and Bram. Singing 'n Swinging.

"Don't Press Your Belly Button." Rappin' Rob. The Rappin' Rob Rap.

"Everybody Knows I Love My Toes." Carfra, Pat. Songs for Sleepyheads and Out-of-Beds.

"Everybody Knows I Love My Toes." Cassidy, Nancy. Kids' Songs Jubilee.

"I'm Alive." Baron, Laura, and Patti Dallas. Songs for the Earth.

"I've Got a Body." Peanutbutterjam. Simply Singable.

"Knickerbocker." Tickle Tune Typhoon. Hug the Earth.

"Noses." Rosenshontz. Rosenshontz Tickles You.

"Shake." Kinnoin, David. Fun-a-Rooey.

"Shakin' It." Parachute Express. Shakin' It!

"Skin." Tickle Tune Typhoon. Hug the Earth.

"S'pose My Toes Were Noses." Paxton, Tom. Suzy Is a Rocker.

"Touch Your Nose." Avni, Fran. Artichokes and Brussel Sprouts.

"Two Thumbs Date." Scruggs, Joe. Ants.

"Wake Up." Guthrie, Woody. Woody's 20 Grow Big Songs.

"Wiggle Your Bones." Parachute Express. Circle of Friends.

"With These Hands." Vitamin L. Singin' in the Key of L.
"Wobbi-Do-Wop." Pease, Tom. Wobbi-Do-Wop.

Animals

"The Bear." Wee Sing Fun 'n' Folk.

Here's a fun, traditional call-and-response song about meeting (and escaping) a bear. It's a good song for a mixed audience of adults and kids. Have them repeat each line. Every four lines, they have to repeat the preceding four lines. The audience will laugh as they sing about jumping up to catch a branch, missing it, and then grabbing it on the way down.
(All)

* "Bear Hunt." Tickle Tune Typhoon. Circle Around.

Although technically not a song, this timeless story-hour activity is a guaranteed hit with the preschool and primary crowd. "Bear Hunt" can also be found on:
    Carfra, Pat. Babes, Beasts, and Birds.
Variations of the activity can be found as:
    "Elephant Hunt." Rappin' Rob. The Rappin' Rob Rap.
    "Going on a Lion Hunt." Parachute Express. Circle of
        Friends.
    "Looking for Dracula." Diamond, Charlotte. 10 Carrot
        Diamond.   *(Ps, Pr)*

"The Circus Song." Muldaur, Maria. On the Sunny Side.

Muldaur sings about all the animals she sees at the circus while carrying water for the elephant. Play the recording and encourage the children to make the sounds of seals barking, lions roaring, bees bumbling, sloths snoring, and more. "The Circus Song" was written by F. Thompson and J. Guernsey. Muldaur's version can also be found on:
    Family Folk Festival.   *(All)*

Animals

"Go into the Night." Miché, Mary. Nature Nuts.

This cumulative song features the sounds of night animals. The simple two-verse structure builds upon coyote, frog, cricket, and owl noises—noises the kids will be happy to provide. This pretty, quiet song is great for campfires. *(All)*

"Going to the Zoo." Paxton, Tom. The Marvellous Toy.

Paxton wrote this, my favorite zoo song. Use it with my favorite zoo picture book, *Sam, Who Never Forgets,* by Eve Rice. Kids will enthusiastically sing "Going to the zoo! zoo! zoo!" "Going to the Zoo" can also be found on:
Cassidy, Nancy. Kids' Songs Jubilee.
The Flyers. Family Hug.
Peter, Paul and Mary. Peter, Paul and Mommy.
Raffi. Singable Songs for the Very Young.
Sharon, Lois and Bram. The Elephant Show Record.
(Ps, Pr)

"I Had a Little Rooster." Buchman, Rachel. Hello, Everybody.

Buchman's version of this traditional, cumulative song is full of sound effects and leaves room for new verses. Here's a good opportunity to pass out all of your animal puppets and feature them in the song. Sing "I had a little rooster" or "I had a little mousie" or if you have an elephant puppet:

I had a little elephant, the elephant pleased me.
I fed my elephant by the old chestnut tree.
My little elephant went [elephant trumpet noise]. . . .

Ask the kids for suggestions when the puppets run out. We had one child suggest a mosquito! ("My little mosquito went buzz buzz buzz.") "I Had a Little Rooster" can also be found as:
"Greenwood Tree." Quackity Yakity Bop.
"Had a Little Rooster." Carfra, Pat. Babes, Beasts, and Birds.
"Had a Little Rooster." Wee Sing Fun 'n' Folk.
"I Had a Rooster." (Pete Seeger) Family Folk Festival.

"I Had a Rooster." Weissman, Jackie. Peanut Butter, Tarzan, and Roosters.

"I Love My Rooster." Dallas, Patti, and Laura Baron. Good Morning Sunshine.

A similar song is the traditional "Bought Me a Cat" found on *Wee Sing Fun 'n' Folk*. Use this song with Paul Galdone's picture book *Cat Goes Fiddle-I-Fee*.

Other variations of this traditional song can be found as:
"Bought Me a Cat." Seeger, Mike and Peggy. American Folk Songs for Children.
"Fiddle Eye Fee." Neat, Roxanne, and David Stoeri. Dance, Boatman, Dance. **(Ps, Pr)**

"If You Love a Hippopotamus." Bishop, Heather. Bellybutton.

This great song lists the advantages of knowing a hippopotamus. Lead the children in a hippo walk while playing the recording. "If You Love a Hippopotamus" was written by Connie Kaldor and can also be found on:
Alsop, Peter. Stayin' Over.
Bethie. Bethie's Really Silly Songs about Animals.
Miché, Mary. Animal Crackers. **(All)**

* "I'm Being Swallowed by a Boa Constrictor." The Chenille Sisters. 1-2-3 for Kids.

Paint a large snake on an old bed sheet. Hold it down by your toes as the snake begins to "swallow" you. Work the sheet up in front of your body as the Chenille Sisters sing (or sing it yourself). The snake will eventually swallow you up, cutting you off in mid-sentence. Written by Shel Silverstein based on his poem from the book *Where the Sidewalk Ends,* it can also be found as "Boa Constrictor" on:
Diamond, Charlotte. Diamond in the Rough.
Peter, Paul and Mary. Peter, Paul and Mommy. **(Ps, Pr)**

"Little White Duck." Kaye, Danny. Danny Kaye for Children.

My colleague Linda Booton uses puppets while singing this song. Use a duck, frog, snake, and bug puppet. Sing this simple tune yourself or hold the puppets up while the recording plays. Kaye's version contains great animal sound effects provided by the backup singers. Joanie Bartels uses a similar arrangement on her version found on *Bathtime Magic*. The song was written by Walt Barrows and Bernard Zanitsky. Other versions of "Little White Duck" can be found on:

> Carfra, Pat. Babes, Beasts, and Birds.
> Ives, Burl. Little White Duck.
> Penner, Fred. The Cat Came Back.
> Quackity Yakity Bop.
> Raffi. Everything Grows. **(Ps, Pr)**

"The Monkey and the Elephant." Cowboy Steff.
The Giving Tree and Other Shel Silverstein Songs.

Shel Silverstein and Baxter Taylor wrote this funny, funny song about an elephant who falls in love with a bee and goes to a monkey for advice. Play the recording and enjoy Cowboy Steff's laid-back singing. The children will join him when he sings "a long time ago" after every verse. **(Pr, I)**

"Monkey See, Monkey Do." The Bumblebeez. Animaland.

See the monkey smile, shake, make a funny face, scratch his head, and more. Whatever the monkey does in this fast-paced song, the children can imitate. This monkey movement song was written by group members Laurie Hedlund, Lianne Sterling, and David Scheffler. **(Ps, Pr)**

"Over in the Meadow." McCutcheon, John. Mail Myself to You.

McCutcheon gives this popular, traditional song a nice, easy rock 'n' roll arrangement.

Over in the meadow in a pond in the sun,
Sat an old mother frog and her little froggy one.
"Hop," said the mother,
"I hopped," said the one.
And they hopped and were happy
In their pond in the sun.

The simple tune can be sung by most folks while holding up the pictures of Paul Galdone's picture book of the same name. Bethie's version from her *Bethie's Really Silly Songs about Numbers* has a nice Caribbean sound. All versions allow the children to chime in with plenty of animal noises. "Over in the Meadow" can also be found on:

Carfra, Pat. Babes, Beasts, and Birds.
Raffi. Baby Beluga. **(All)**

"The Pets." Berman, Marcia. Marcia Berman Sings Malvina Reynolds' Rabbits Dance.

"The Pets" is Malvina Reynolds's tongue-twisting love poem to pets. There are nonsensical descriptions of what the various pets do (eat flip-floppers or livers or periwinkles). The kids will giggle at the silly names given to the pets (Miss Feedle Faddle, McGonigle, MacMurdie, Klonkey, and Dolally). The kids can make the appropriate animal noises at the end of each chorus. "The Pets" can also be found on:

Ungar, Jay, and Lyn Hardy. A Place to Be. **(Ps, Pr)**

"A Place in the Choir." Tickle Tune Typhoon. Hug the Earth.

Tickle Tune Typhoon's version of this famous Bill Staines song is funny and full of sound effects. If you have a lot of animal puppets, pass them out to the kids and have the puppets sing along with the recording. Show Staines's picture book *All God's Critters Got a Place in the Choir*, illustrated by Margot Zemach. All in all, this is my favorite animal song. Sometimes listed as "A Place in the Choir" and sometimes as "All God's Critters," it can also be found on:

Abell, Timmy. The Farmer's Market.
Grammer, Red. Down the Do-Re-Mi.

McCutcheon, John. Howjadoo.
Miché, Mary. Nature Nuts.
Nagler, Eric. Fiddle Up a Tune.
Quackity Yakity Bop.
Staines, Bill. The Happy Wanderer.   *(All)*

"Sittin' Down to Eat." Harley, Bill. Big Big World.

This song is similar to Mirra Ginsburg's picture book *Mushroom in the Rain*. In the song, several animals crowd into Harley's house. When an itty-bitty caterpillar crawls in, the whole house goes boom. Read Ginsburg's book, then play the recording. The kids will chime in on the chorus. "Sittin' Down to Eat" was written by Harley with help from his son Noah.

(All)

* "When Cows Get Up in the Morning." Carfra, Pat. Babes, Beasts, and Birds.

Here is a simple call-and-response camp song that can go on forever. The singer calls "When cows get up in the morning, they always say 'good day.'/'Moo, moo,' that's how they say 'good day.' " Carfra also features ape, hyena, snake, parrot, and baby noises. Let the kids contribute their own verses. Encourage them to think of non-animal noises (helicopters, telephones).   *(Ps, Pr)*

"Wolf Party." The Singing Rainbow Youth Ensemble. Head First and Belly Down.

Nancy Schimmel and Candy Forest have written one of the few children's songs that portrays wolves in a natural way and not as villains. The song describes the need for young wolves to practice their howling. Your children can join in with their own howls.   *(All)*

"You Can't Make a Turtle Come Out." Grandma's Patchwork Quilt.

Cathy Fink sings this version of the Malvina Reynolds song. If your library or school can afford the Folkmanis turtle puppet, use it with this song. (See appendix B for ordering information.) The head pulls into the shell. As the song is sung, coax the shy turtle out of its shell. Use your thumb hiding in your fist as a less expensive alternative. "You Can't Make a Turtle Come Out" can also be found on:

> Berman, Marcia. Marcia Berman Sings Malvina
> > Reynolds' Rabbits Dance.
> Gemini. Pulling Together.
> Miché, Mary. Earthy Tunes.
> Sharon, Lois and Bram. In the Schoolyard.
> Ungar, Jay, and Lynn Hardy. A Place to Be.   *(Ps)*

Here are more great songs about animals:

Alligators and Crocodiles

"Al the Alligator." Miché, Mary. Animal Crackers.

"Allen Gator." Paxton, Tom. Balloon-Alloon-Alloon.

"Alligator in the Elevator." Charette, Rick. Alligator in the Elevator.

"The Alligator Waltz." Bishop, Heather. Bellybutton.

"Alvin the Alligator." Rockow, Corrine. I Sing Every Day of My Life.

"The Crocodile." Wee Sing Silly Songs.

"Crocodile's Toothache." Silverstein, Shel. Where the Sidewalk Ends.

"Deep in the Jungle." Scruggs, Joe. Deep in the Jungle.

"Never Smile at a Crocodile." McCornack, Mike and Carleen. Sunshine Cake.

"Never Smile at a Crocodile." Penner, Fred. Poco.

"The Smile on the Crocodile." Sharon, Lois and Bram. All the Fun You Can Sing!

"The Smile on the Crocodile." Sharon, Lois and Bram. Great Big Hits.

"The Smile on the Crocodile." Sharon, Lois and Bram. Singing 'n Swinging.

"Susie and the Alligator." Fink, Cathy. When the Rain Comes Down.

"Susie and the Alligator." Fink, Cathy, and Marcy Marxer. A Cathy and Marcy Collection for Kids.

"Suzy and the Alligator." Neat, Roxanne, and David Stoeri. Dance, Boatman, Dance.

"Swampbaby Stomp." The Bumblebeez. Animaland.

Armadillos

"Little Armadillos." Foote, Norman. Foote Prints.

Bears

"Baby Bear's Chicken Pox." Avni, Fran. Artichokes and Brussel Sprouts.

"The Bear That Snores." Roth, Kevin. Unbearable Bears.

"The Bear Went over the Mountain." Monet, Lisa. Jump Down.

"The Bear Went over the Mountain." Roth, Kevin. Oscar, Bingo, and Buddies.

"The Bear Went over the Mountain." Wee Sing Silly Songs.

"Dance with the Bears." Bethie. Bethie's Really Silly Songs about Animals.

"Grizzly Bear." Wee Sing Fun 'n' Folk.

"Just Let Me Sleep (The Bear)." The Bumblebeez. Animaland.

"One Shoe Bear." Rosenshontz. It's the Truth.

"The Show Biz Bear." Roth, Kevin. Unbearable Bears.

"That Bear Drives Me Crazy." Roth, Kevin. Unbearable Bears.

"Three Bears." The Flyers. Family Hug.

"Unbearable Bears." Roth, Kevin. Unbearable Bears.

"Waltzing with Bears." Herdman, Priscilla. Stardreamer.

"Waltzing with Bears." Neat, Roxanne, and David Stoeri. Hummin' Words.

"Waltzing with Bears." Roth, Kevin. Daddysongs.

Bulls

"Ferdinand the Bull." Feinstein, Michael. Pure Imagination.

"The Little Black Bull." Rosenthal, Phil. Chickens in the Garden.

"The Little Black Bull." The Seeger Family. Animal Folk Songs for Children.

Camels

"Cameling." Chapin, Tom. Billy the Squid.

"Camille, the Kissing Camel." Buckner, Janice. Everybody's Special.

"No One Knows for Sure." Alsop, Peter. Wha'd'ya Wanna Do?

Cats

"As Long as We're Together." Parachute Express. Happy to Be Here.

"Big Old Cat." Lewis, Shari. Lamb Chop's Sing-Along, Play-Along.

"Billy Bop Cat." McCornack, Mike and Carleen. Beasties, Bumbershoots, and Lullabies.

"The Cat Came Back." Miché, Mary. Kid's Stuff.

"The Cat Came Back." Penner, Fred. The Cat Came Back.

"The Cat Came Back." Penner, Fred. Collections.

"The Cat Came Back." Sharon, Lois and Bram. Singing 'n Swinging.

"The Cat Came Back." Trout Fishing in America. Big Trouble.

"The Cat Came Back (Again)." Penner, Fred. Poco.

"Cat Song." Gemini. Two of a Kind.

"Dagger." Lonnquist, Ken. A Little Dreamin'.

"Don Gato." Phipps, Bonnie. Dinosaur Choir.

"Five Cool Cats." Bethie. Bethie's Really Silly Songs about Numbers.

"I Sold My Cat." Lonnquist, Ken. Welcome 2 Kenland.

"I Wanna Purple Kitty for My Birthday, Mom." Diamond, Charlotte. Diamonds and Dragons.

"Kitty Cat Man." Bethie. Bethie's Really Silly Songs about Animals.

"The Kitty Cats' Party." Carfra, Pat. Lullabies and Laughter with the Lullaby Lady.

"Max the Cat." The Chenille Sisters. The Big Picture.

"My Cat Can." Colleen and Uncle Squaty. Colleen and Uncle Squaty.

"My Kitty Kat." Miché, Mary. Animal Crackers.

"No, You May Not Eat My Kitty." Kinnoin, Dave. Daring Dewey.

"Porky." Charette, Rick. Where Do My Sneakers Go at Night?

"Three Little Kittens." Sharon, Lois and Bram. Mainly Mother Goose.

"Tickles the Cat." Monet, Lisa. Jump Down.

Cows

"Barnyard Talk." Arnold, Linda. Happiness Cake.

"The Bellcow." Nagler, Eric. Improvise with Eric Nagler.

"Beulah Merryweather Moo." McCornack, Mike and Carleen. Beasties, Bumbershoots, and Lullabies.

"Cows Night Out." (Karan and the Musical Medicine Show) Early Ears: Songs Just for 4 Year Olds.

"Cows on the Moon." The Bumblebeez. Animaland.

"Did You Feed My Cow?" Sharon, Lois and Bram. Smorgasbord.

"I'd Like to Be a Cowgirl." Fink, Cathy. Grandma Slid down the Mountain.

"Kiss a Cow." Crow, Dan. Oops!

"Many Cows." Pease, Tom. Boogie Boogie Boogie.

"Oh, the Bell Cow." Neat, Roxanne, and David Stoeri. The Bell Cow Swing.

Dogs *see* page 74

Dolphins

"Dolphin Dance." Tickle Tune Typhoon. Hearts and Hands.

"Dolphin Drummers." Pirtle, Sarah. Magical Earth.

"Dolphins." Charette, Rick. Chickens on Vacation.

"The Dolphins and the Mermaids." Lonnquist, Ken. A Little Dreamin'.

"Pelorous Jack." Pirtle, Sarah. Two Hands Hold the Earth.

Donkeys

"Erie Canal." Grammer, Red. Red Grammer's Favorite Sing Along Songs.

"Hold 'Em Joe." Penner, Fred. A House for Me.

"Hold 'Im Joe." Sharon, Lois and Bram. Smorgasbord.

"Mules." Wee Sing Silly Songs.

"Riding on a Donkey." Rosenthal, Phil. Comin' Round the Mountain.

"Sweetly Sings the Donkey." Wee Sing Sing-Alongs.

"Ting-a-Lay-O." Cassidy, Nancy. Kids' Songs.

"Tingalayo." Parachute Express. Shakin' It!

"Tingalayo." Raffi. One Light, One Sun.

"Tingalayo." Raffi. Raffi in Concert with the Rise and Shine Band.

"Tingalayo." Sharon, Lois and Bram. Great Big Hits.

"Tingalayo." Sharon, Lois and Bram. One Elephant, Deux Elephants.

"Whoa Mule." Neat, Roxanne, and David Stoeri. Hummin' Words.

Elephants

"Chew a Cherry." Lonnquist, Ken. Welcome 2 Kenland.

"The Elephant March." The Bumblebeez. Animaland.

"Elephant Song." Cappelli, Frank. Pass the Coconut.

"Engelbert the Elephant." Paxton, Tom. The Marvellous Toy.

"In the Jungle." Lonnquist, Ken. A Little Dreamin'.

"In the Jungle." Rockow, Corrine. I Sing Every Day of My Life.

"Little Elephants." Monet, Lisa. Jump Down.

"The Monkey and the Elephant." Cowboy Steff. The Giving Tree and Other Shel Silverstein Songs.

"One Elephant." Carfra, Pat. Lullabies and Laughter with the Lullaby Lady.

"One Elephant." Sharon, Lois and Bram. Great Big Hits.

"One Elephant, Deux Elephants." Sharon, Lois and Bram. One Elephant, Deux Elephants.

"One Elephant Went Out to Play." Sharon, Lois and Bram. The Elephant Show Record.

"Purple Elephant." Nagler, Eric. Come On In.

"Un Elephante." Sharon, Lois and Bram. In the Schoolyard.

"When I See an Elephant Fly." Nagler, Eric. Fiddle Up a Tune.

Foxes

"The Fox." Carfra, Pat. Lullabies and Laughter with the Lullaby Lady.

"The Fox." Cassidy, Nancy. Kids' Songs.

"The Fox." Colleen and Uncle Squaty. Colleen and Uncle Squaty.

"The Fox." Ives, Burl. The Best of Burl's for Boys and Girls.

"The Fox." Neat, Roxanne, and David Stoeri. Hummin' Words.

"The Fox." Penner, Fred. Ebeneezer Sneezer.

"The Fox." Peter, Paul and Mary. Peter, Paul and Mommy, Too.

"The Fox's Dance." Pirtle, Sarah. Two Hands Hold the Earth.

Frogs see page 103

Giraffes

"A Giraffe Can Laugh." Paxton, Tom. Suzy Is a Rocker.

"Joshua Giraffe." Raffi. Baby Beluga.

"Too Tall Tilly." Bethie. Bethie's Really Silly Songs about Numbers.

Gnus

"Gned the Gnu." Rosen, Gary. Tot Rock.

Goats

"Bill Grogan's Goat." Miché, Mary. Kid's Stuff.

"Bill Grogan's Goat." Wee Sing Silly Songs.

"The Goat." Ives, Burl. Little White Duck.

"A Kid and a Goat." Foote, Norman. If the Shoe Fits.

"Pap's Billygoat." McCutcheon, John. Howjadoo.

Gorillas

"Gorilla Feet." Kinnoin, Dave. Fun-a-Rooey.

Groundhogs

"Ground Hog/Oh Ground Hog." Neat, Roxanne, and David Stoeri. The Bell Cow Swing.

Hippopotamuses

"Hippo Hooray!" Arnold, Linda. Happiness Cake.

"Hippopotamus Rock." Rosenshontz. Rosenshontz Tickles You.

"Otto the Hippo." Penner, Fred. Collections.

"Otto the Hippo." Penner, Fred. A House for Me.

Horses

"A Happy Horse." Crow, Dan. A Friend, A Laugh, A Walk in the Woods.

"Horsey, Horsey." Rosenthal, Phil. The Paw Paw Patch.

"I Have a Little Pony." Carfra, Pat. Songs for Sleepyheads and Out-of-Beds.

"Listen to the Horses." Raffi. More Singable Songs.

"Magic Horse." Arnold, Linda. Make Believe.

"The Magic Horse." Pirtle, Sarah. Two Hands Hold the Earth.

"Merry-Go-Round." Parachute Express. Shakin' It!

"The Pony." Charette, Rick. Alligator in the Elevator.

"Ride a Cock Horse." Dallas, Patti, and Laura Baron. Playtime Parade.

"Stewball." Miché, Mary. Animal Crackers.

"The Tennessee Stud." Watson, Doc. Doc Watson Sings Songs for Little Pickers.

"The Trail Ride." Chapin, Tom. Moonboat.

Kangaroos

"Diggery Kangaroo." Bethie. Bethie's Really Silly Songs about Animals.

"Kangaroo Hip Hop." The Bumblebeez. Animaland.

"Tie Me Kangaroo Down Sport." Cassidy, Nancy. Kids' Songs Jubilee.

Lions

"Going on a Lion Hunt." Parachute Express. Circle of Friends.

"Wimoweh." Grammer, Red. Red Grammer's Favorite Sing Along Songs.

Lizards

"Ivana the Iguana." Bethie. Bethie's Really Silly Songs about Animals.

"The Little Lizard." Roth, Kevin. Dinosaurs, Dragons, and Other Children's Songs.

"Lizards." Banana Slug String Band. Adventures on the Air Cycle.

Mice

"As Long as We're Together." Parachute Express. Happy to Be Here.

"Hickory, Dickory, Dock." Wee Sing.

"Little Bunny Foo Foo." Wee Sing Silly Songs.

"Little Miss Mousie." Bethie. Bethie's Really Silly Songs about Animals.

"Little Mouse Creeping." Monet, Lisa. Circle Time.

"Little Rabbit Foo-Foo." Sharon, Lois and Bram. Great Big Hits.

"Little Rabbit Foo-Foo." Sharon, Lois and Bram. Mainly Mother Goose.

"Morton Simon." McCornack, Mike and Carleen. Beasties, Bumbershoots, and Lullabies.

"The Mouse and the Clock." Colleen and Uncle Squaty. Colleen and Uncle Squaty.

"The Tailor and the Mouse." Ives, Burl. Little White Duck.

"Three Blind Mice." (Jonathan Edwards) Grandma's Patchwork Quilt.

"Three Blind Mice." Quackity Yakity Bop.

"Three Blind Mice." Roth, Kevin. Oscar, Bingo, and Buddies.

"Three Blind Mice." Sharon, Lois and Bram. Mainly Mother Goose.

"Three Blind Mice." Wee Sing Sing-Alongs.

"A Trio of Myopic Rodents." Rappin' Rob. The Rappin' Rob Rap.

Monkeys

"The Aba Daba Honeymoon." Bartels, Joanie. Sillytime Magic.

"Aba Daba Honeymoon." Bethie. Bethie's Really Silly Songs about Animals.

"The Aba Daba Honeymoon." Sharon, Lois and Bram. Singing 'n Swinging.

"Abba Dabba Honeymoon." The Chenille Sisters. The Big Picture.

"Deep in the Jungle." Scruggs, Joe. Deep in the Jungle.

"Here Sits a Monkey." Raffi. Corner Grocery Store.

"The Monkey Song." Noah, Tim. In Search of the Wow Wow Wibble Woggle Wazzie Woodle Woo!

"Monkey Talk." Lonnquist, Ken. A Little Dreamin'.

"The Monkeys' Baseball Game." Paxton, Tom. Balloon-Alloon-Alloon.

"No One Knows for Sure." Alsop, Peter. Wha'd'ya Wanna Do?

"Tale about a Tail." Tracey, Paul. The Rainbow Kingdom.

Moose

"I'm Proud to Be a Moose." (David Van Ronk) American Children.

"I'm Proud to Be a Moose." Van Ronk, David. Peter and the Wolf.

Opossums

"Brother Possum." Pirtel, Sarah. Two Hands Hold the Earth.

"Raccoon and Possum." The Seeger Family. Animal Folk Songs for Children.

"Raccoon's Got a Bushy Tail." Seeger, Pete. Stories and Songs for Children.

Otters

"Head First and Belly Down." The Singing Rainbow Youth Ensemble. Head First and Belly Down.

Pigs

"Big Pig." The Bumblebeez. Animaland.

"The Boogie Woogie Pig." Nagler, Eric. Fiddle Up a Tune.

"Eight Piggies in a Row." Raffi. Everything Grows.

"Everybody Ought to Be a Pig." Bethie. Bethie's Really Silly Songs about Animals.

"The Fat Pig Waltz." The Van Manens. Healthy Planet, Healthy People.

"Four Wet Pigs." Brown, Greg. Bathtub Blues.

"A Jolly Old Pig." Carfra, Pat. Songs for Sleepyheads and Out-of-Beds.

"Little Pig." The Seeger Family. Animal Folk Songs for Children.

"The Little Pig." Seeger, Mike and Peggy. American Folk Songs for Children.

"Little Piggy." Roth, Kevin. The Secret Journey.

"The Old Sow." The Seeger Family. Animal Folk Songs for Children.

"The Old Sow." Sharon, Lois and Bram. One Elephant, Deux Elephants.

"The Old Sow Song." Penner, Fred. Ebeneezer Sneezer.

"The Old Woman and Her Pig." Buchman, Rachel. Hello Rachel! Hello Children!

"Pigs." Quackity Yakity Bop.

"The Skinny Pig." Crow, Dan. Oops!

"The Sow Song." Carfra, Pat. Babes, Beasts, and Birds.

"The Sow Took the Measles." Ives, Burl. Little White Duck.

"Susannah's a Funny Old Man." Sharon, Lois and Bram. All the Fun You Can Sing!

"Susannah's a Funny Old Man." Sharon, Lois and Bram. Great Big Hits.

"Susannah's a Funny Old Man." Sharon, Lois and Bram. Sing A to Z.

"Tails and Trotters." Roth, Kevin. Daddysongs.

"This Little Piggy." Scruggs, Joe. Traffic Jams.

"Three Little Pigs." Avni, Fran. Artichokes and Brussel Sprouts.

"The Three Little Pigs Blues." Greg and Steve. Playing Favorites.

"Three Piggy Jive." Nagler, Eric. Come On In.

"Who's Afraid of the Big Bad Wolf?" Rosenshontz. Share It.

"The Wonderful Pigtown Fair." Paxton, Tom. Suzy Is a Rocker.

Platypuses

"Gus the Platypus." Shontz, Bill. Animal Tales.

Porcupines

"With a Porcupine." Kinnoin, Dave. Dunce Cap Kelly.

Rabbits

"Babies and Bunnies." Kinnoin, Dave. Fun-A-Rooey.

"Big-Eyed Rabbit." Carfra, Pat. Lullabies and Laughter with the Lullaby Lady.

"Here Is a Bunny." Monet, Lisa. Circle Time.

"Little Bunny Foo-Foo." Wee Sing Silly Songs.

"Little Cabin in the Woods." Wee Sing.

"Little Peter Rabbit." Wee Sing.

"Little Rabbit Foo-Foo." Sharon, Lois and Bram. Great Big Hits.

"Little Rabbit Foo-Foo." Sharon, Lois and Bram. Mainly Mother Goose.

"Little Rabbit, Where's Your Mammy?" Fink, Cathy. Grandma Slid down the Mountain.

"Mister Rabbit." O'Brien, Bruce. In My Family's House.

"Mister Rabbit." The Seeger Family. Animal Folk Songs for Children.

"Mister Rabbit." Seeger, Pete. Stories and Songs for Children.

"Mr. John, the Rabbit." Carfra, Pat. Lullabies and Laughter with the Lullaby Lady.

"Mr. Rabbit." Ives, Burl. Little White Duck.

"Mr. Rabbit." Roth, Kevin. The Sandman.

"My Dog Treed Rabbit." Nagler, Eric. Fiddle Up a Tune.

"Oh, John the Rabbit." Seeger, Mike and Peggy. American Folk Songs for Children.

"Ol' John the Rabbit." Sharon, Lois and Bram. Mainly Mother Goose.

"Old Mister Rabbit." Seeger, Mike and Peggy. American Folk Songs for Children.

"Old Molly Hare." Nagler, Eric. Improvise with Eric Nagler.

"Old Molly Hare." Neat, Roxanne, and David Stoeri. Hummin'
Words.

"Old Molly Hare." Seeger, Mike and Peggy. American Folk
Songs for Children.

"Rabbits Dance." Berman, Marcia. Marcia Berman Sings
Malvina Reynolds' Rabbits Dance.

"The Turtle and the Hare." Roth, Kevin. The Secret Journey.

"Wascawy Wabbit." (Lois LaFond) Early Ears: Songs Just for
5 Year Olds.

"Wascawy Wabbit." LaFond, Lois. One World.

Raccoons

"One Cold and Frosty Morning." Seeger, Mike and Peggy.
American Folk Songs for Children.

"Raccoon and Possum." The Seeger Family. Animal Folk Songs
for Children.

"Raccoon's Got a Bushy Tail." Seeger, Pete. Stories and Songs
for Children.

Rhinoceroses

"Don't Be Rude to a Rhinoceros." Paxton, Tom. Peanut Butter
Pie.

"My Rhinoceros." Drake, David HB. Kid-Stuff.

"My Rhinoceros." Miché, Mary. Animal Crackers.

"Rhino!" Lonnquist, Ken. A Little Dreamin'.

Seals

"Can't Be an Elephant." The Singing Rainbow Youth Ensemble.
Head First and Belly Down.

"Play with Me (The Seal)." The Bumblebeez. Animaland.

Sheep

"Baa, Baa, Black Sheep." Monet, Lisa. Circle Time.

"Baa, Baa, Black Sheep." Raffi. Singable Songs for the Very Young.

"The Big Sheep." The Seeger Family. Animal Folk Songs for Children.

"Little Bo-Peep." Rosenthal, Phil. Comin' Round the Mountain.

"Mary Had a Little Lamb." Sharon, Lois and Bram. Mainly Mother Goose.

"Tender Shepherd." McCutcheon, John. Howjadoo.

"Wooly Old Wally Walloo." McCornack, Mike and Carleen. Sunshine Cake.

Skunks

"Little Skunk." Miché, Mary. Earthy Tunes.

"The Little Skunk's Hole." Wee Sing Silly Songs.

"Three Little Smelly Skunks." Rappin' Rob. The Rappin' Rob Rap.

Snakes

"Green and Yeller." Miché, Mary. Kid's Stuff.

"Sam the Snake." Bethie. Bethie's Really Silly Songs about Animals.

"Sneaky Snakes." Miché, Mary. Kid's Stuff.

"Spiders and Snakes." Miché, Mary. Earthy Tunes.

Squirrels

"Angus McTavish." Neat, Roxanne, and David Stoeri. Dance, Boatman, Dance.

"Hop, Old Squirrel." Seeger, Mike and Peggy. American Folk Songs for Children.

"Peep Squirrel." Shake It to the One That You Love the Best.

"Seven Silly Squirrels." Avni, Fran. Daisies and Ducklings.

Tigers

"A Tiger Never Changes His Stripes." The Bumblebeez. Animaland.

Turtles

"Sea Turtle Memories." The Singing Rainbow Youth Ensemble. Head First and Belly Down.

"The Turtle." Carfra, Pat. Lullabies and Laughter with the Lullaby Lady.

Whales

"Baby Beluga." Cassidy, Nancy. Kids' Songs.

"Baby Beluga." (Raffi) A Child's Celebration of Song.

"Baby Beluga." Raffi. Baby Beluga.

"Baby Beluga." Raffi. Raffi in Concert with the Rise and Shine Band.

"Baby Beluga." Raffi. Raffi on Broadway.

"Rubber Blubber Whale." Diamond, Charlotte. Diamonds and Dragons.

"Rubber Blubber Whale." McCutcheon, John. Howjadoo.

"Sarah the Whale." Sharon, Lois and Bram. All the Fun You Can Sing!

"Sarah the Whale." Sharon, Lois and Bram. Happy Birthday.

"Seaweed Jam." Pirtle, Sarah. Two Hands Hold the Earth.

"Sing a Whale Song." Chapin, Tom. Moonboat.

"That Quiet Place." Pirtle, Sarah. Two Hands Hold the Earth.

"The Whale." Ives, Burl. Little White Duck.

"Whale Song." Rogers, Sally. Piggyback Planet.

"Who Did Swallow Jonah?" Wee Sing Silly Songs.

Wolves

"The Three Little Pigs Blues." Greg and Steve. Playing Favorites.

"Who's Afraid of the Big Bad Wolf?" Rosenshontz. Share It.

Worms

"200 Worms on the Sidewalk." Walker, Mary Lu. The Frog's Party.

"Earthworm Boogie." Baron, Laura, and Patti Dallas. Songs for the Earth.

"Lots of Worms." Sharon, Lois and Bram. Stay Tuned.

"Nobody Likes Me." Wee Sing Silly Songs.

"Squirming Worms." Cassidy, Nancy. Kids' Songs Jubilee.

Zebras

"Counting Zebras." Block, Cathy. Timeless.

Bathtime

"Bathtub Blues." Brown, Greg. Bathtub Blues.

The singer gets so dirty that he has to take a bath every night. Then he spends so much time in the tub that he turns into a duck. Greg Brown wrote this call-and-response bathtime song with a group of sixth-graders. **(Pr, I)**

"Bubble Bath." Rory. I'm Just a Kid.

Rory co-wrote this doo-wop bubble bath song with Tom Guernsey. Let the children blow soap bubbles to set the mood. Play the recording and let the children join the background singers when they sing "bu-bu-bu-bubble bath." "Bubble Bath" can also be found on:
Bartels, Joanie. Bathtime Magic. **(All)**

"Cleano." Neat, Roxanne, and David Stoeri. Hummin' Words.

Children can act out scrubbing their faces, ears, hair, knees, and feet while listening to this Woody Guthrie song. Guthrie's own version, "Clean O," can be found on:
Guthrie, Woody. Woody's 20 Grow Big Songs.

A similar feel-good-about-taking-a-bath song is Raffi's composition "Bathtime," found on his *Everything Grows* recording. Again, children can make scrubbing motions while listening to the recording. "Bathtime" can also be found on:
Bartels, Joanie. Bathtime Magic. **(Ps)**

* "Head, Shoulders, Knees, and Toes." Bartels, Joanie. Bathtime Magic.

The traditional version of this popular song directs children to point to various parts of their bodies. Bartels effectively adapts this into a fun bath song by having the children make washing motions on their heads, shoulders, knees, toes, eyes, ears, mouths, and noses. The traditional version can be found on:
Cassidy, Nancy. Kids' Songs 2.

Dallas, Patti, and Laura Baron. Playtime Parade.

Raffi. Rise and Shine. (Raffi's version, "Tête, Epaules," is in French and English.) **(Ps)**

"I Love Mud." Charette, Rick. Alligator in the Elevator.

Here is a song about kids who need to take a bath because they are wild about mud. Charette sings about children who do the backstroke wearing white outfits in mud, eat mud creations, and who get lost in mud puddles for twenty-five years. The chorus is extemely catchy.

Mud, mud, I love mud.
I'm absolutely, positively wild about mud.
I can't go around it, I've got to go through it,
Beautiful, fabulous, super-duper mud.

"I Love Mud" is a good companion song for the picture book *Mud Puddle* by Robert Munsch. **(All)**

* "I'm a Dirty Kid." Buchman, Rachel. Hello Rachel! Hello Children!

Buchman doesn't mention baths in her song, but these kids

can surely use one. Buchman celebrates her dirty cheeks, neck, and feet in this catchy call-and-response song. The kids brag about their dirtiness and then shout "But I don't care!" over and over. Children (and their parents) remembered this song (in a positive way) months after we sang it at our Family Storytimes. *(All)*

"Looby Loo." Sharon, Lois and Bram. One Elephant, Deux Elephants.

Many folks don't know that this traditional song is thought to be about taking a hot bath on a Saturday night. "You put your right hand in" to check if the water is too hot. When you find that it is too hot, "you take your right hand out." The song can also be found as:

> "Here We Go Loopty-Loo." Little Richard. Shake It All About.
>
> "Looby Loo." Rosenthal, Phil. The Paw Paw Patch.
>
> "Looby Loo." Wee Sing.
>
> "Loop 'D Loo." Greg and Steve. We All Live Together, Vol. 1.
>
> "Loop De Loo." Shake It to the One That You Love the Best. *(All)*

"Rub-a-Dub." Palmer, Hap. More Baby Songs.

Palmer wrote this fun bath song designed for children to pantomine scrubbing various body parts. He starts at the top with the face, cheeks, and ears ("keep your eyes shut") and works down to the tummy, legs, and feet. "Rub-a-Dub" can also be found on:

> Bartels, Joanie. Bathtime Magic. *(Ps)*

"Singing in the Tub." The Chenille Sisters. 1-2-3 for Kids.

The Chenille Sisters like to sing, swim, sit, and blurble in the tub. The children can add their own verses and blurble with the recording by moving their fingers over their lips. This fun bath song can be enhanced with bubble soap and other props such as a long-handled back washer, washcloth, and bath toys. "Singing in the Tub" was written by group members Connie Huber and Grace Morand. **(Ps)**

"There's a Hippo in My Tub." Bartels, Joanie. Bathtime Magic.

The narrator knows she should take a bath but tells Mom she can't because of the hippo, penguin, and crocodile in the tub. Play the recording while bouncing puppets of the above animals in a plastic infant tub. "There's a Hippo in My Tub" was written by Bartels and Chris Ryne. **(Ps, Pr)**

Here are more great songs about bathtime:

"Away, Mommy, Away." Abell, Timmy. The Farmer's Market.

"Bathtub Blues." Scruggs, Joe. Bahamas Pajamas.

"The Bathtub Song." Arnold, Linda. Make Believe.

"Boogie Woogie Washrag Blues." Palmer, Hap. Peek-a-Boo.

"Don't Drink the Water in the Bathtub." Atkinson, Lisa. The One and Only Me.

"If You're Gonna Be a Grub." Harley, Bill. You're in Trouble.

"I'm Gonna Stay in the Bathtub 'Til the Soap Disappears." Kahn, Si. Good Times and Bed Times.

"In That Bubble." Crow, Dan. Oops!

"Miss Lucy." Shake It to the One That You Love the Best.

"Miss Lucy." Sharon, Lois and Bram. All the Fun You Can Sing!

"Miss Lucy." Sharon, Lois and Bram. Stay Tuned.

"Rubber Blubber Whale." Diamond, Charlotte. Diamonds and Dragons.

"Rubber Blubber Whale." McCutcheon, John. Howjadoo.

"The Shower Song." Sprout, Jonathan. On the Radio.

Bedtime

"The Bear That Snores." Roth, Kevin. Unbearable Bears.

A poor bear wants to sleep with the narrator because of a strange noise in the dark. The noise turns out to be the bear itself snoring! Kids will be able to snore away during the chorus. "The Bear That Snores" was written by Roth and can also be found on:

Roth, Kevin. Travel Song Sing Alongs. **(All)**

"Children under the Bed." Phipps, Bonnie. Monsters' Holiday.

Monster children are fearful that human children are hiding under their beds. The song is a natural pairing with Robert Crowe's picture book *Clyde Monster*, about another young monster afraid of human children. "Children under the Bed" was written by Dave Kinnoin and Jimmy Hamner.

(Ps, Pr)

"Eight O'Clock Midnight Snack." Kahn, Si. Good Times and Bed Times.

Various family members sneak into the kitchen for an evening snack. The food starts to pile up on the table. A simple glass of milk is followed by half a slice of bread, a marshmallow sandwich, a bowl of soup, an omelette, a milkshake, a leg of lamb, turkey, and a three-layer cake. If you're ambitious, make food felt pieces and watch the children's eyes pop out as they see the food added on a felt table one after another. Liz and Dick Wilmes's *Felt Board Fun* has a table pattern and several various food patterns. "Eight O'Clock Midnight Snack" was written by Kahn. **(All)**

"I Can't Sleep." (Kitty Gill) Early Ears: Songs Just for 5 Year Olds.

Excuses, excuses. I've heard them all at bedtime from my own four children. Now these same excuses are listed in this song by Kitty Gill. The child in the song can't go to sleep

because of an itchy nose, loud rain, and a moon that's too
bright. The song is a wonderful companion to Russell
Hoban's picture book *Bedtime for Francis,* in which a young
badger has several excuses for not going to bed.   *(Ps, Pr)*

"It's Time to Go to Bed." Charette, Rick. Chickens on Vacation.

Charette calls out, "It's time to go to bed," to which your
audience can whine back, "Do I have to go to bed?" The
ending has a fun twist when the adults get tired and the
kids tell them "It's time to go to bed!" "It's Time to Go to
Bed" was written by Charette.   *(All)*

"Late at Night When I'm Hungry." Charette, Rick. Bubble Gum and Other Songs for Hungry Kids.

Food tastes so much better in the middle of the night. To
get to the kitchen, the kids have to sneak past their parents'
bedroom, stomp past brother's room, and squeak past the
baby's room. After they're done eating, they have to go back
the same way. This highly participative song closes with
everyone saying goodnight to the stars, the moon, the fish,
their toes, and their stomachs. "Late at Night When I'm
Hungry" was written by Charette.   *(All)*

"Quit That Snorin'." Roth, Kevin. The Sandman.

Who's snoring? Roth and kids wander around the house
trying to locate the source of all that noise. Roth wonders if
it's his teddy bear. The kids will have lots of opportunities
to make snoring sounds during the course of the recording.
Create a bedtime atmosphere by turning out the lights and
walking around the room with a flashlight. (Be aware of
very young children who might be too frightened if all of
the lights are turned off.) So who's the culprit in the end?
Daddy! "Quit That Snorin' " was written by Roth. *(Ps, Pr)*

"Sleep, Sleep." Rosenshontz. Share It.

Rosenshontz gives the children a chance to be the parents
and chant, "Sleep, sleep/Ya gotta go to sleep," over and over

and over. As the child, Gary Rosen gives plenty of excuses why he can't go to sleep (monsters under the bed, homework). *(All)*

"There's a Werewolf under My Bed." Troubadour. On the Trail.

Here's a great match for the picture book *I Was a Second Grade Werewolf* by Daniel Pinkwater. The song has a catchy chorus the kids can quickly learn. "There's a Werewolf under My Bed" was written by Judy Steinbergh and Victor Cockburn. A similar song is Si Kahn's "Under the Bed" on his *Good Times and Bed Times* recording. Both songs go well with Mercer Mayer's book *There's an Alligator under My Bed*. *(Pr, I)*

"Time to Sleep." Marxer, Marcy. Jump Children.

I didn't include lullabies in this book since they don't easily fit into a library story program or school curriculum. But I couldn't resist highlighting one of the prettiest lullabies created in recent years. Check it out and use it at home on your infants. Written by Marxer, it is also beautifully covered on:

>   Cassidy, Nancy. Kids' Songs Sleepyheads.
>   Herdman, Priscilla. Stardreamer. *(Ps)*

"What's That Noise?" Kahn, Si. Good Times and Bed Times.

This eerie song comes complete with spooky organ noises. The kids can scream at the end of the recording. I usually ask them, with a mischievous wink, if they hadn't always wanted to scream in the library or classroom. "What's That Noise?" was written by Kahn. *(Pr)*

"Where's My Pajamas?" Sharon, Lois and Bram. The Elephant Show Record.

And where are the pillows, slippers, blankets, and everything else one needs for bedtime? Have the children add their favorite bedtime items (teddy bears, night-lights) to the pattern established in this simple song. "Where's My

Pajamas" can also be found on:
> Seeger, Pete. Abiyoyo and Other Story Songs for
> Children.
> Sharon, Lois and Bram. All the Fun You Can Sing!
> **(Ps, Pr)**

"Whole Bed." Scruggs, Joe. Bahamas Pajamas.

Scruggs starts off with the traditional "There were five in the bed and the little one said, 'Roll over.' " When the last one rolls out of bed, Scruggs breaks into "I've got the whole mattress to myself" to the tune of "He's Got the Whole World in His Hands." Sharon, Lois and Bram use this same ending on their "Ten in the Bed" from *The Elephant Show Record*. Traditional versions of the song can be found as "Ten in the Bed" or "Roll Over" on:
> Monet, Lisa. Jump Down.
> Penner, Fred. Fred Penner's Place.
> Wee Sing Silly Songs. **(Ps, Pr)**

Here are more great songs about bedtime:

"Bedtime Round." Chapin, Tom. Billy the Squid.

"Bobo's Bedtime." Parachute Express. Over Easy.

"Dreamtime Rendezvous." Grammer, Red. Down the Do-Re-Mi.

"Gingerbread Man." Scruggs, Joe. Bahamas Pajamas.

"Go to Sleep, You Little Creep." Alsop, Peter. Stayin' Over.

"Grandma's Sleeping in My Bed Tonight." Scruggs, Joe. Late Last Night.

"I Can't Sleep." Paxton, Tom. Suzy Is a Rocker.

"I Don't Wanna Go to Bed." Craig 'n Co. Morning 'n Night.

"I'm Not Gonna Go to Sleep." Kahn, Si. Good Times and Bed Times.

"I'm Not Tired." Carfra, Pat. Babes, Beasts, and Birds.

"It's Time to Go to Bed." Roth, Kevin. The Sandman.

"No More Bedtimes." Kahn, Si. Good Times and Bed Times.

"Over Easy." Parachute Express. Over Easy.

"Slumber Party." Wellington, Bill. WOOF Hits Home.

"Slumber Party." Wellington, Bill. WOOF's Greatest Bits.

"Sunday Morning." Rosenshontz. Uh-Oh.

"Time for Bed." Rory. Make-Believe Day.

"Under Your Bed." Scruggs, Joe. Traffic Jams.

"Underneath the Covers with My Flashlight On." Kahn, Si. Good Times and Bed Times.

"Wake You in the Morning." Pelham, Ruth. Under One Sky.

"You Might as Well Go to Sleep." Brown, Greg. Bathtub Blues.

Birds

* **"Baby Bird." Wee Sing.**

> This short, short traditional song has plenty of movement. Very young children can act out a baby bird leaving its egg and learning to fly (only to fall down, down, down).   **(Ps)**

"Billy Magee Magaw." Rogers, Sally. What Can One Little Person Do?

> Your kids can join the kids on the recording and sing the traditional "Billy Magee Magaw" to the tune of "When Johnny Comes Marching Home." Those who don't want to sing can add "Caw! Caw!" sound effects.   **(Ps, Pr)**

"Butts Up." Banana Slug String Band. Slugs at Sea.

> My favorite song titles in this book are Waylon Jennings's "All of My Sisters Are Girls" and "Butts Up" by Banana Slug String Band. In order to drink their "marsh mud shake," ducks feed on the water "butts up." The children will giggle throughout the playing of this recording as they quack and shout (what else?) "Butts up!" If you have a duck puppet, tip its tail up in the air for each "Butts up!" Banana Slug String Band has found a fun way to convey the importance of preserving our wetlands.   **(All)**

* "Chickadee." Monet, Lisa. My Best Friend.

You can make up your own fingerplay actions to the words of this traditional backwards counting song. Here are mine:

Five little chickadees	(Hold up five fingers.)
peeking in the door	(Peek through fingers.)
one flew away	(Flap hands like wings.)
and then there were four	(Hold up four fingers.)

Monet adds her own verse when all five chickadees return to build a nest in her hair. A calypso version of the song called "Five Little Chickadees" can be found on:

Sharon, Lois and Bram. Mainly Mother Goose.   **(Ps)**

"Five Little Ducks." Buchman, Rachel. Hello Everybody.

Buchman does a nice job of addressing this song to the very young by telling them how to make a fingerplay out of the lyrics. The song makes a good felt activity with one mother duck and five baby ducks. Felt patterns can be found in Judy Sierra's *The Flannel Board Storytelling Book*. Nancy Tafuri's picture book *Have You Seen My Duckling?* and Raffi's book *Five Little Ducks* make good companions to this traditional song. "Five Little Ducks" can also be found on:

Monet, Lisa. Circle Time.
Raffi. Raffi in Concert with the Rise and Shine Band.
Raffi. Rise and Shine.

A similar song is the popular "Six Little Ducks," which can also be sung with fingerplay actions. Use the same felt characters you made for "Five Little Ducks" (just add another baby duck). This traditional song can be found on:

Avni, Fran. Daisies and Ducklings.
Bartels, Joanie. Bathtime Magic.
Raffi. More Singable Songs.
Rosenthal, Phil. The Paw Paw Patch.   **(Ps)**

"Kookaburra." Miché, Mary. Earthy Tunes.

This traditional song about the Australian bird is often done as a round. Miché's version has an added verse about sitting

on an electric wire. "Kookaburra" can also be found on:
Dallas, Patti, and Laura Baron. Playtime Parade.
Quackity Yakity Bop.
Wee Sing around the World.
Wee Sing Sing-Alongs. *(All)*

"Migratin'." Rogers, Sally. What Can One Little Person Do?

Ten bluebirds are having fun until different weather clues direct them to fly south for the winter. Make ten felt bluebirds and a tree. *Felt Board Fun* by Liz and Dick Wilmes has several generic bird and tree patterns. Remove the bluebirds from the felt board one by one as Rogers sings this backwards counting song. The children will shout out the numbers as Rogers sings "and then there were ____!" "Migratin'" was written by Rogers. *(Ps)*

"Polly the Parrot." Grunsky, Jack. Waves of Wonder.

Who better to lead a call-and-response song than a parrot? Instead of the parrot repeating everything the children say, the roles are reversed. Polly leads the children through a recitation of musical instruments ("the oompah-oompah tuba"), taking a bath, and throwing an animal party. Use a parrot puppet for Polly if you have one (the song is still a lot of fun if you don't). "Polly the Parrot" was written by Grunsky. *(Ps, Pr)*

* "Three Craw." Sharon, Lois and Bram. The Elephant Show Record.

Bram teaches this Scottish folksong to a live audience. "Craw" is what a crow is called in Scotland. Make three simple, felt crows out of triangles and circles. Use a large upside-down triangle for the crow body, a small triangle for the tail, a small circle for the head, and a tiny orange or yellow triangle for the beak. Remove the "craws" one by one during the course of the song. The tune is very simple. Just follow Bram's example. *(All)*

Here are more great songs about birds:

"Bahamas Pajamas." Scruggs, Joe. Bahamas Pajamas.

"Birdies Ball." Carfra, Pat. Babes, Beasts, and Birds.

"Bluebird, Bluebird." Sharon, Lois and Bram. Mainly Mother Goose.

"Bye Bye Dodo." Chapin, Tom. Billy the Squid.

"The Crow That Wanted to Sing." Paxton, Tom. Balloon-Alloon-Alloon.

"A Duck Named Earl." (Phil Rosenthal) Grandma's Patchwork Quilt.

"Five Little Sparrows." Diamond, Charlotte. My Bear Gruff.

"Fly High (The Eagle)." The Bumblebeez. Animaland.

"The Little House." Raffi. Everything Grows.

"Penguins on Parade." The Bumblebeez. Animaland.

"Robin in the Rain." Raffi. Singable Songs for the Very Young.

"This Song Is for the Birds." Staines, Bill. The Happy Wanderer.

"The Ugly Duckling." (Danny Kaye) A Child's Celebration of Song.

"The Ugly Duckling." Greg and Steve. We All Live Together, Vol. 4.

"The Ugly Duckling." Penner, Fred. A House for Me.

"Young Robin." Brown, Greg. Bathtub Blues.

Birthdays

"The Backwards Birthday Party." Chapin, Tom. Zag Zig.

The birthday cake gets eaten first, everyone blindfolds the donkey and pins the tail on the kids, the ice cream is hot, and the birthday boy gives all of his presents to his guests. By the end of the day, he is one year younger. Play the recording and enjoy the nonsense. Ask the children what their backwards birthday party would be like. "The

Backwards Birthday Party" was written by Chapin and John Forster. **(Pr)**

"Birthday Cake." Parachute Express. Sunny Side Up.

The kids can act out baking a birthday cake by cracking the eggs, pouring the sugar, stirring the milk and flour, counting to ten while the cake is in the oven, spreading the frosting, and finally blowing out the candles. This cumulative song goes well with the picture book *Benny Bakes a Cake* by Eve Rice. "Birthday Cake" was written by group member Peter Dergee. **(Ps, Pr)**

"Happy Birthday, Happy Birthday." Nagler, Eric. Come On In.

Not the traditional version, but one that could quickly become a classic. This very pretty and moving birthday song is set to the music of Franz Lehar's "The Merry Widow Waltz." Nagler patiently teaches the song to his audience.

> *Happy birthday, happy birthday,*
> *We love you.*
> *Happy birthday and may all your dreams come true.*
> *When you blow out the candles*
> *One light stays aglow.*
> *That's the lovelight in your eyes*
> *Where e'er you go.*

This same version of "Happy Birthday, Happy Birthday" can also be found on:
Chapin, Tom. Moonboat.
Sharon, Lois and Bram. Happy Birthday. **(All)**

"P.A.R.T.Y." Janet and Judy. Good Clean Fun.

This infectious song describes the excitement that comes with having a birthday party. From the arrival of the friends to the eating of the chocolate cake, a birthday is a child's moment in the spotlight. The book *The Berenstain Bears and Too Much Birthday* by Jan and Stan Berenstain is a nice cautionary tale to use with the song. In the book, Sister gets caught up in too much birthday excitement. "P.A.R.T.Y." was written by Janet and Judy Robinson with Steve Trytten. It can also be found on:

Bartels, Joanie. Jump for Joy.   *(Pr, I)*

"The Unbirthday Song." Sharon, Lois and Bram. Happy Birthday.

Throw a "Happy Unbirthday" party for everyone who doesn't have a birthday that day. Share several birthday stories and songs with games. This Disney song makes a great opening song for such an occasion. It is a very short song that wishes a very merry unbirthday to all the children present, one by one. "The Unbirthday Song" was written by Mack David, Al Hoffman, and Jerry Livingston and can also be found on:

Feinstein, Michael. Pure Imagination.   *(Ps, Pr)*

Here are more great songs about birthdays:

"Birthday Hallelujah." Sharon, Lois and Bram. Happy Birthday.

"Birthday Song." Rosenthal, Phil. Comin' round the Mountain.

"The Birthday Song." Wozniak, Doug. Hugs and Kisses.

"Cut the Cake." McCutcheon, John. Howjadoo.

"Great Big Box." Paxton, Tom. Peanut Butter Pie.

"Happy Birthday Jig." Sharon, Lois and Bram. Happy Birthday.

"Happy Birthday to You." Rosenthal, Phil. Comin' round the Mountain.

"Happy Birthday to You." Sharon, Lois and Bram. Happy Birthday.

"I Wanna Purple Kitty for My Birthday, Mom." Diamond, Charlotte. Diamonds and Dragons.

"It's Your Birthday." Buckner, Janice. Everybody's Special.

"Skateboard." Scruggs, Joe. Deep in the Jungle.

"Waiting." Walker, Mary Lu. The Frog's Party.

Brotherhood/Sisterhood

"Brothers and Sisters." Grammer, Red. Down the Do-Re-Mi.

Powerful! Teach the children the easy-to-follow chorus and sing with the recording. The song opens and closes with greetings from children around the world. Over time, this song will be recognized as one of the best. "Brothers and Sisters" was written by Red and Kathy Grammer. **(All)**

"Love Grows One by One." Pease, Tom. I'm Gonna Reach.

Pease uses sign language while acting out the chorus of this song.

> *Love grows one by one*
> *Two by two*
> *And four by four.*
> *Love grows 'round like a circle*
> *And comes back knockin' at your front door.*

"Love Grows One by One" was written by Carol Johnson. It can also be found on:
Herdman, Priscilla. Daydreamer. **(All)**

"One World." LaFond, Lois. One World.

Kids repeat LaFond's statements of unity to a very lively, Latino beat. One world, one love, one heart begin this litany of hope. The song ends with the phrase "one world" sung in French, Russian, Chinese, and Spanish. LaFond's version can also be found on:
Early Ears: Songs Just for 6 Year Olds. **(Pr, I)**

"The Other Side of the World." Pirtle, Sarah. Magical Earth.

Pirtle sings about turning the world around and seeing who lives on "the other side of the world." Point to the various countries on a globe as Pirtle sings about Braulio in Santiago, Li-min in Canton, Miriam in Jerusalem, Kuraluk in the Arctic, Ahmed in Cairo, Chipo in Soweto, and several other children of the world. "The Other Side of the World" was written by Pirtle. **(Pr, I)**

"Part of the Family." LaFond, Lois. One World.

LaFond asks who are her neighbors, sisters, and brothers. The children on the tape respond that they are her neighbors, sisters, and brothers. LaFond then asks who is her neighbor in French, Russian, Spanish, and Japanese. The children respond in the same languages. LaFond's version can also be found on:

Early Ears: Songs Just for 6 Year Olds. **(Pr, I)**

"Walk a Mile." Vitamin L. Walk a Mile.

Here it is! Jan Nigro's "Walk a Mile" is my all-time favorite children's song. It encourages children to see the world through other people's eyes. The chorus is powerful and exciting. Teach it to the children. Versions that are as equally powerful can be found on:

Harley, Bill. Big Big World.

Pease, Tom. Wobbi-Do-Wop. **(Pr, I)**

"When the Rain Comes Down." Fink, Cathy. When the Rain Comes Down.

Bob Devlin's song is another one of the greatest children's songs ever written. When the rain comes down, when the sun shines, when a flower blooms, and when a baby smiles—it is for us all. "When the Rain Comes Down" can also be found on:

Fink, Cathy, and Marcy Marxer. A Cathy and Marcy Collection for Kids.

Herdman, Priscilla. Daydreamer.

Grunsky, Jack. Children of the Morning.

Pease, Tom. Wobbi-Do-Wop. **(All)**

Here are more great songs about brotherhood and sisterhood:

"All the Children." Paxton, Tom. Balloon-Alloon-Alloon.

"All the People." Foote, Norman. If the Shoe Fits.

"American Children." (Richie Havens). American Children.

"Building Bridges." The Van Manens. Healthy Planet, Healthy People.

"Family." Rory. Make-Believe Day.

"Family Feeling." Vitamin L. Walk a Mile.

"The Family Tree." The Van Manens. We Recycle.

"I Live in a City." Berman, Marcia. Marcia Berman Sings Malvina Reynolds' Rabbits Dance.

"I'm on My Way." Harley, Bill. 50 Ways to Fool Your Mother.

"It Takes a Lot of People." Pease, Tom. I'm Gonna Reach.

"Kids' Peace Song." Alsop, Peter. Take Me with You.

"Kids' Peace Song." Miché, Mary. Peace It Together.

"Kids' Peace Song." (Peter Alsop) Peace Is the World Smiling.

"Like Me and You." Raffi. One Light, One Sun.

"Like Me and You." Raffi. Raffi in Concert with the Rise and Shine Band.

"Like Me and You." Raffi. Raffi on Broadway.

"Listen." Grammer, Red. Teaching Peace.

"Look to the People." Pelham, Ruth. Under One Sky.

"Mama's Kitchen." Raffi. Evergreen, Everblue.

"Miles of Smiles." Bartels, Joanie. Jump for Joy.

"My Rainbow Race." Seeger, Pete. Family Concert.

"One World Family." Abell, Timmy. Play All Day.

"People Are a Rainbow." Vitamin L. Walk a Mile.

"The Picnic of the World." Chapin, Tom. Mother Earth.

"Tear down the Walls." Vitamin L. Singin' in the Key of L.

"To Everyone in All the World." Raffi. Baby Beluga.

"Under One Sky." Harley, Bill. 50 Ways to Fool Your Mother.

"Under One Sky." Pelham, Ruth. Under One Sky.

"Walls and Bridges." Pirtle, Sarah. Magical Earth.

"We All Sing with the Same Voice." Monet, Lisa. My Best Friend.

"World Citizen." Pease, Tom. Boogie Boogie Boogie.

"A World United." Vitamin L. Singin' in the Key of L.

Clothing

* "The Best Old Hat." Peanutbutterjam. Simply Singable.

The singer asks the children if they remembered to wash their face, brush their teeth, button up their shirts, and put their pants on straight. The children respond that they did indeed do all of that and could they now please get their hats. Add your own verses to this silly song. "The Best Old Hat" was written by Eileen Packard. *(Pr)*

"Black Socks." Harley, Bill. Monsters in the Bathroom.

This old camp favorite explains why black socks never need washing. It is fairly easy for older kids to learn either as a straight rendition or as a round.

> *Black socks, they never need washing.*
> *The longer you wear them, the stronger they get.*
> *Sometimes I think I should change them,*
> *But something inside me keeps saying*
> *Not yet, not yet, not yet.* *(I)*

"Critters in My Clothes." Peanutbutterjam. Incredibly Spreadable.

Different animals crawl, hop, or fly into Eileen Packard's shoes, pants, shirt, socks, sweater, suit, and pajamas. Listen to how effectively she encourages the kids in her audience to supply the animals. Some of their hilarious choices include an elephant in her sweater and a frog in her suit. This pattern song was written by Packard. *(Ps, Pr)*

"Hey, Hey, Put It On." Peanutbutterjam. Peanutbutterjam Goes to School.

Paul Recker of Peanutbutterjam sings that you should put

on your white undies, yellow socks, green shirt, blue pants, brown shoes, red vest, orange coat, black boots, and purple hat. The kids sing a scatlike "ba-doo-ba-doo" after each line. The song ends with a big "Oh yeah!" This Eileen Packard song has good felt possibilities. There are several clothing and human figure patterns in the Wilmes's *Felt Board Fun* book. **(Ps, Pr)**

"I Can Put My Clothes On by Myself." Palmer, Hap. Peek-a-Boo.

Forget what anyone says—orange pants do go well with a pink shirt and if one sock is white and red and the other is blue—it doesn't matter. The important thing is that you got dressed all by yourself. Palmer's original song matches well with Shigeo Watanabe's picture book *How Do I Put It On?*

(Ps)

"I Had an Old Coat." Rockow, Corrine. I Sing Every Day of My Life.

Not only is this song a great match for the picture book *The Wonderful Shrinking Shirt* by Leone Castelle Anderson, but it is also a catchy tune with an infectious chorus. Based on an old folk story, the tune follows a coat that is torn and turned into a jacket. The jacket becomes worn and turned into a shirt and so on until it is only a button (and then that becomes gone!). "I Had an Old Coat" was written by Paul Kaplan and can also be found on:

Sharon, Lois and Bram. Happy Birthday. **(All)**

* "I Want to Wear." Buchman, Rachel. Hello Everybody.

"I want to wear my" (fill in the blank). That's pretty much the content of this simple song. The young kids love it.

(Ps)

"Once I Saw Three Goats." Sharon, Lois and Bram. Singing 'n Swinging.

"Once I saw three goats and they were wearing coats." And

some bees who were wearing skis, frogs in clogs, and llamas in pajamas. Add to the formula. This very short song has the potential to go on and on, depending on the children's imaginations. Sing the song after reading Judi Barrett's picture book *Animals Should Definitely Not Wear Clothing.* *(All)*

"Polka Dots, Checks, and Stripes." Parachute Express. Happy to Be Here.

This lively song is about an individual who always wears— what else? She even has a cat named Tiger and a dog named Spot. There are plenty of chances for the kids to sing "polka dots, checks, and stripes" in the song. To enliven your sessions, wear polka dots, checks, and stripes yourself. "Polka Dots, Checks, and Stripes" was written by group members Stephen Michael Schwartz and Janice Hubbard. *(All)*

"When My Shoes Are Loose." Fink, Cathy, and Marcy Marxer. Help Yourself.

Sound effects of clothing (zip-zip, button-button) are scattered throughout the song. There are several more sound effects, such as pouring milk (glub-glub) and washing hands (wisha-washa). The song, written by Bill Brennan, has a Woody Guthrie feel. Play the recording after reading Jonathan London's picture book *Froggy Gets Dressed,* which has similar sound effects. *(Ps, Pr)*

Here are more great songs about clothing:

"The Dressing Song." Feinstein, Michael. Pure Imagination.

"Eleven Gallon Hat." The Flyers. Family Hug.

"The Guy with the Polka Dot Tie." Grammer, Red. Red Grammer's Favorite Sing Along Songs.

"(Hip-Hopping, Be-Bopping) Super-Duper Dancing Sneakers." Scooter. Miles of Smiles.

"Holes in the Knees." Troubadour. Can We Go Now?

"I Lost My Shoes." LaFond, Lois. One World.

"I Wonder Where's My Underwears." Peanutbutterjam. Incredibly Spreadable.

"The Laundry." Diamond, Charlotte. Diamond in the Rough.

"Mary Wore Her Red Dress." Seeger, Mike and Peggy. American Folk Songs for Children.

"The Mitten Song." Walker, Mary Lu. The Frog's Party.

"A Modest Proposal (Long Underwear)." Rockow, Corrine. I Sing Every Day of My Life.

"Pink Polka Dot Underwear." Lonnquist, Ken. Welcome 2 Kenland.

"Pyjamarama." Grunsky, Jack. Waves of Wonder.

"Sneakers." Tickle Tune Typhoon. Circle Around.

"The Sock Monster." (Glenn Bennett) Early Ears: Songs Just for 6 Year Olds.

"Underwear." Polisar, Barry Louis. Family Concert.

"Underwear." Polisar, Barry Louis. Teacher's Favorites.

"The Washing Machine." The Chenille Sisters. The Big Picture.

"What Are You Wearing?" Wee Sing.

"What You Gonna Wear?" Fink, Cathy, and Marcy Marxer. Help Yourself.

"Where Do My Sneakers Go at Night?" Charette, Rick. Where Do My Sneakers Go at Night?

Color

"Brown Bear, Brown Bear, What Do You See?" Greg and Steve. Playing Favorites.

Greg and Steve's song is based on Bill Martin's famous picture book of the same title. In fact, the words are used directly from the book with Martin's permission. If you're not familiar with this modern classic book, check it out right away. Brown bear sees a redbird who sees a yellow duck who sees a blue horse who sees other colorful animals. Hold the illustrations up while playing the recording. The music was adapted by Greg Scelsa. **(Ps)**

"The Crazy Traffic Light." Rappin' Rob. The Rappin' Rob Rap.

What would you do if you came to a traffic light that turned blue? Or orange? Or pink? Rappin' Rob instructs the children to bark like a dog, oink like a hog, hop like a bunny, or make a loud roar, depending on the color. "The Crazy Traffic Light" was written by Rob Reid.   **(Ps, Pr)**

"De colores." Pirtle, Sarah. Two Hands Hold the Earth.

Pirtle sings the first part of this traditional song in Spanish and then repeats it in English. The colors of the fields, the birds, and the sky are celebrated in the song. "De colores" can also be found on:

    Raffi. One Light, One Sun.

    Tickle Tune Typhoon. Hearts and Hands.   **(All)**

* "If You're Wearing Any Red." Rappin' Rob. The Rappin' Rob Rap.

"If you're wearing any red, put your shoe on your head . . . If you're wearing any yellow, turn your body into Jello . . ." and so on. Listen to the tape and find out what the kids must do if they're wearing blue, pink, or white. Follow Rappin' Rob's silly instructions or make up your own rhymes. "If You're Wearing Any Red" was written by Rob Reid. Jack Grunsky's "Let's Paint a Picture," from *Children of the Morning,* is another song that directs children to perform an activity if they see a certain color.   **(All)**

"Jenny Jenkins." Neat, Roxanne, and David Stoeri. Dance, Boatman, Dance.

David Stoeri asks "Jenny" (Roxanne Neat) if she'll wear a certain color in this traditional American folk song. Jenny always has an excuse for why a color doesn't suit her. Kids will love to learn the long, nonsensical chorus "Find me a fiddle-faddle, tiddle-toddle, seek-a-double, use-a-cause-a-roll to find me," or its many variations. Similar versions can be found on:

Garcia, Jerry, and David Grissman. Not for Kids Only.

Miché, Mary. Kids Stuff.

Sharon, Lois and Bram. Great Big Hits.

Sharon, Lois and Bram. Smorgasbord.

Wee Sing Fun 'n' Folk. *(All)*

"Mixing Colors." Rosen, Gary. Tot Rock.

Ellen Stoll Walsh's picture book *Mouse Paint* is a great companion for this song. Read the book, then play Rosen's recording. Borrow theater light gels from your local high school's or university's theater department. Combine the colors of the gels to make new colors. Another fun picture book about mixing colors is *Little Blue and Little Yellow* by Leo Lionni. And another fun song about mixing colors is "Red and Blue and Yellow Too" by Cheech Marin on *My Name Is Cheech the School Bus Driver*. *(Ps, Pr)*

"Rainbow 'round Me." Pelham, Ruth. Under One Sky.

Kids select an object and describe its color. The children in the song see a red car, a purple flower, a yellow sun, and a blue sky. Make a felt window. Ask the children what they imagine they see through the window. Make colorful felt patterns of these objects and place them in the window. This cumulative song was written by Pelham. *(Ps, Pr)*

Here are more great songs about colors:

"Color Song." Parachute Express. Feel the Music.

"Colors/colores." LaFond, Lois. I Am Who I Am!

"I Can Sing a Rainbow." Penner, Fred. Happy Feet.

"I Know the Colors of the Rainbow." Jenkins, Ella. I Know the Colors of the Rainbow.

"Parade of Colors." Palmer, Hap. Can a Cherry Pie Wave Goodbye?

"Put a Little Color on You." Palmer, Hap. Can a Cherry Pie Wave Goodbye?

"Rainbow Kingdom." Tracey, Paul. The Rainbow Kingdom.

"Rainbow of Colors." Greg and Steve. We All Live Together, Vol. 5.

"Sing a Rainbow." The Flyers. Family Hug.

Dinosaurs

"Dicky Dicky Dinosaur." Diamond, Charlotte. Diamonds and Dragons.

Diamond has written a short, rap-like chant with sound effects. Someone steps on Dicky's tail and the children yell "Yipes!" When the T-Rex is after Dicky, the kids yell "Run!" And when Dicky roars, the kids roar back. Lots of fun.

(Ps, Pr)

"Dinosaur and the Progress of Man." Foote, Norman. Foote Prints.

A dinosaur awakens and asks a farmer about the progress of man. The dinosaur is curious about a certain animal (a tractor), a volcano (a factory), and a bird (an airplane). The dinosaur decides he has seen enough and goes back to sleep for another million years. This song is a good companion to the picture book *We're Back* by Hudson Talbott. *(Pr)*

"Dinosaurs." Tickle Tune Typhoon. Circle Around.

This song describes the great size of some dinosaurs and how they behaved. The kids can stomp their feet, show their teeth, roar, and move their heads like dinosaurs.

(Pr, I)

"If I Had a Dinosaur." Raffi. More Singable Songs.

Imagine what you could do with your very own dinosaur. Raffi suggests taking it to the zoo, looking inside a cloud, and going to grandma's house. Play the recording after reading Syd Hoff's *Danny and the Dinosaur*. "If I Had a

Dinosaur" was written by Raffi, Debi Pike, and Bert and Bonnie Simpson. **(Ps)**

"I'm a 3-Toed, Triple-Eyed, Double-Jointed Dinosaur." Phipps, Bonnie. Dinosaur Choir.

Barry Louis Polisar wrote the best children's song about dinosaurs. Phipps recorded the best version. Write the words to the chorus so the audience can sing along .

> *I'm a three-toed, triple-eyed, double-jointed dinosaur*
> *with warts up and down my back.*
> *I eat shiny automobiles,*
> *tow trucks, and airplanes.*
> *I love to munch on railroad tracks.*

"I'm a 3-Toed, Triple-Eyed, Double-Jointed Dinosaur" can also be found on:

Polisar, Barry Louis. Family Concert.

Polisar, Barry Louis. Old Dog, New Tricks. **(Pr, I)**

"Tyrannosaurus Rex." (Peter Schickle) American Children.

Peter Schickle (also known as P.D.Q. Bach) wrote and sang this lively, funny account of why the mean *Tyrannosaurus* doesn't scare him. The kids can sing "Tyrannosaurus Rex" over and over again at the end. **(All)**

"When I Was a Dinosaur." The Chenille Sisters. 1-2-3 for Kids.

Turn this fun number into a call-and-response song. This is one of the few songs from the dinosaur's (or "future fossil fuel's") point of view. "When I Was a Dinosaur" was written by David Egan and Larry Armer. It can also be found on:

Trout Fishing in America. Big Trouble. **(All)**

Here are more great songs about dinosaurs:

"At the Dinosaur Baseball Game." Arnold, Linda. Peppermint Wings.

"Crazy for Dinosaurs." Rosenshontz. Family Vacation.

"Dinosaur." Troubadour. Can We Go Now?

"Dinosaur Bones." Phipps, Bonnie. Dinosaur Choir.

"Dinosaur Choir." Phipps, Bonnie. Dinosaur Choir.

"Dinosaur Tooth Care." Phipps, Bonnie. Dinosaur Choir.

"Dinosaurs at Play." Paxton, Tom. Peanut Butter Pie.

"Do the Dino Rap." Grunsky, Jack. Children of the Morning.

"Please Don't Bring a Tyrannosaurus Rex to Show and Tell."
Scruggs, Joe. Late Last Night.

"There's a Dinosaur Knocking at My Door." Arnold, Linda.
Happiness Cake.

"We Are the Dinosaurs." Trout Fishing in America. Big Trouble.

Dogs

* "Bingo." Greg and Steve. We All Live Together, Vol. 4.

Many children are familiar with this traditional song about
a farmer and his dog. Each time a verse is sung, a letter from
the name "Bingo" is dropped and often substituted with a
clap. Try replacing the missing letters with a bark or growl
like Greg and Steve. "B-I-woof-woof-woof." You can use
other animals. "There was a farmer had a cow and Bingo [or
Daisy or Elsie] was her name-o. B-I-moo-moo-moo."
"Bingo" can also be found on:
Monet, Lisa. Jump Down.

Quackity Yakity Bop.

Roth, Kevin. Oscar, Bingo, and Buddies.

Sharon, Lois and Bram. Sing A to Z.

Wee Sing. *(All)*

"Bobo and Fred." Rosenshontz. Rock 'n' Roll Teddy Bear.

This catchy song is about a smart dog and his not-too-smart
owner, Fred. Play the recording while manipulating a dog
puppet. The recording will provide the dialogue. Then read

Phil Bolsta's poem "Freddie" from Bruce Lansky's *Kids Pick the Funniest Poems*. The poem is about a smart dog that does his master's homework. **(Pr)**

* **"Do Your Ears Hang Low?" Sharon, Lois and Bram. Stay Tuned.**

This is by far the best recording of this traditional song with Sharon, Lois and Bram adding verses for eyes, nose, and mouth. While this song doesn't specifically mention dogs, you'll look like a dog when you put a pair of tights on your head as described on Rappin' Rob's version from *The Rappin' Rob Rap*. "Do Your Ears Hang Low?" can also be found on:

Bartels, Joanie. Sillytime Magic.

Cassidy, Nancy. Kids' Song Jubilee.

Roth, Kevin. Oscar, Bingo, and Buddies.

Wee Sing Silly Songs. **(Ps, Pr)**

* **"Doggie." Grammer, Red. Can You Sound Just like Me?**

Kids can make sniffing, licking, snoring, and howling noises. Try singing the song without the recording. The tune is simple and the words are easy to learn. **(Ps)**

"Dogs." Phipps, Bonnie. Monsters' Holiday.

Phipps does a memorable job with this hilarious song. The gritty production makes you feel like you're groveling in the dirt with a dog. There are several opportunities for the kids to go "woof" and "arf" as they listen to the tape. The original by Dan Crow, who wrote the song, is just as good. His version can be found on:

Crow, Dan. Oops! **(All)**

"How Much Is That Doggie in the Window?" Sharon, Lois and Bram. Stay Tuned.

How does this trio come up with such imaginative arrangements? The background chorus comprises one member singing "Bull! Dog!" while another sings "Chihuahua!" and the third singing "Terrier!"—one voice on top of the other.

Split your audience into three groups, teach each group to sing one of the above parts, and sing the melody over their voices. Beautiful! Try it for a school assembly. The same version can also be found on:

Sharon, Lois and Bram. Great Big Hits. ***(All)***

"I Wanna Be a Dog." Diamond, Charlotte. 10 Carrot Diamond.

Barry Louis Polisar wrote this very popular song recorded by several artists. Diamond's version is perhaps the easiest to follow, but any of the versions work just as well. Diamond performs this song in concert wearing ear muffs made to look like dog ears. "I Wanna Be a Dog" can also be found on:

Alsop, Peter. Wha'd'ya Wanna Do?
Bethie. Bethie's Really Silly Songs about Animals.
Cassidy, Nancy. Kids' Songs Jubilee.
Miché, Mary. Animal Crackers.
Polisar, Barry Louis. Family Concert.
Polisar, Barry Louis. Old Dog, New Tricks. ***(All)***

"I've Got a Dog and My Dog's Name Is Cat." Polisar, Barry Louis. Family Concert.

And Polisar's cat is named "Dog" and his fish is named "Bird" and his bird's name is "Fish." Don't even try to top Polisar's live version. Just sit back and laugh with the kids. "I've Got a Dog and My Dog's Name Is Cat" can also be found on:

Polisar, Barry Louis. Old Dog, New Tricks.

Another song about funny pet names is "Rock and Roll Dog," sung by Glenn Bennett on *Early Ears: Songs Just for 5 Year Olds*. This song is about a dog named "Rock and Roll" and a cat named "Sandy Claws." ***(All)***

* "My Dog Rags." Cassidy, Nancy. Kids' Songs 2.

This is a fun "get-up-and-move-around" activity song. Cassidy's version contains a book that describes the

motions. This song can also be found as "Rags" on:
Sharon, Lois and Bram. Great Big Hits.
Sharon, Lois and Bram. Smorgasbord.   *(Ps, Pr)*

"You'll Be Sorry." Chapin, Tom. Billy the Squid.

Play the recording and listen as Chapin warns his dog about
a cat with a stripe (a skunk), a fly in a yellow jacket (a bee),
and a groundhog with spines (a porcupine). The kids can
join the chorus with its drawn-out "You'll be sor-r-r-y!"

(All)

Here are more great songs about dogs:

"Bark in the Dark." Kahn, Si. Good Times and Bed Times.

"The Bee and the Pup." Wee Sing Fun 'n' Folk.

"Best of Companions." Chapin, Tom. Zag Zig.

"Dog Songs." Livingston, Bob. Open the Window.

"The Dog with Two Tails." Paxton, Tom. Balloon-Alloon-
Alloon.

"The Doggie Duet." (Fred Miller) Early Ears: Songs Just for 4
Year Olds.

"Fred." Paxton, Tom. The Marvellous Toy.

"Have a Little Dog." Seeger, Mike and Peggy. American Folk
Songs for Children.

"Little Dog Named Right." The Seeger Family. Animal Folk
Songs for Children.

"Mr. Jones's Dog." Bennett, Glenn. I Must Be Growing.

"Not Much of a Dog." Feinstein, Michael. Pure Imagination.

"Old Dog." Rosenthal, Phil. Chickens in the Garden.

"Our Dog Bernard." Miché, Mary. Animal Crackers.

"Our Dog Bernard." Polisar, Barry Louis. Old Dog, New Tricks.

"Polly." The Flyers. Your Smile.

"Puppy Dog Blues." Bennett, Glenn. I Must Be Growing.

"Raining Cats and Dogs." (Lois LaFond) Early Ears: Songs Just
for 5 Year Olds.

"Raining Cats and Dogs." LaFond, Lois. One World.

"She's My Dog." The Van Manens. We Recycle.

"Wild Dog on Our Farm." Pease, Tom. Boogie Boogie Boogie.

"Zinger." Lonnquist, Ken. A Little Dreamin'.

Ecology

"Garbage." Rogers, Sally. Piggyback Planet.

> This popular song, written by William Steele, is about, well, garbage. The children can quietly chant "garbage, garbage, garbage" at various spots. "Garbage" can also be found on:
> Miché, Mary. Nature Nuts.
> Rosenshontz. Share It.   **(Pr, I)**

"Junk Round." Rogers, Sally. Piggyback Planet.

> Rogers has written an ecological version of that old favorite "Fish and Chips and Vinegar," also known as "One Bottle of Pop." Instead of singing "one bottle of pop," Rogers now sings "one bottle returned." "Fish and chips and vinegar" is changed to "toxic waste and chemicals." The sentiment of the verse, "Don't dump your junk in my backyard," remains the same. This song makes a good school assembly presentation.   **(Pr, I)**

"Listen to the Water." Schneider, Bob. Listen to the Children.

> What do you see by the waterside? Schneider sings about seeing birds, flowers, ducks, and fish. Ask the children what else they might see and add their ideas to the pattern. "Listen to the Water," written by Schneider, contains several sound effects. This is one of those "head hummers" —a catchy song you'll be humming in your head long after you've heard it. "Listen to the Water" can also be found on:
> Avni, Fran. Daisies and Ducklings.
> Diamond, Charlotte. My Bear Gruff.   **(All)**

"Over in the Endangered Meadow." Rogers, Sally. Piggyback Planet.

Rogers has again added ecological concerns to a traditional song. This time she addresses endangered animals in a new version of "Over in the Meadow." Rogers sings about several animals and their habitats, including whales, pandas, peregrine falcons, ospreys, ferrets, shrikes, gila monsters, and leatherback turtles. **(I)**

"Recycle Around." Cappelli, Frank. Take a Seat.

Here's an interesting idea. Write a round about recycling as Cappelli does here. Since rounds recycle verses of a song, why not recycle a recycle song? Lyrics are included for those ambitious enough to teach children the various parts. Otherwise, sit back and enjoy the recording. **(I)**

"Someone's Gonna Use It." Chapin, Tom. Family Tree.

Chapin and John Forster have written wonderful descriptions of how air and water travel around the world. They speculate that the water you brushed your teeth with used to be in a snowball that an Eskimo threw. And the air you used in a sneeze might have one time been blown out of a whale's spout. Ask the children to use their imaginations to describe where their water and air might have once traveled. Another song that talks about water traveling around the world is Ken Whiteley's "I Heard the Water Singing" from *All of the Seasons*. **(Pr, I)**

"We're Kids That Recycle." Baron, Laura, and Patti Dallas. Songs for the Earth.

The commonsense benefits of recycling are stressed in this song. The kids can echo "We're kids that recycle" during the chorus. Another upbeat recycle song is "Recycle It" by Michael Mish on *A Kid's Eye View of the Environment*. **(All)**

Here are more great songs about ecology:

"The Air." Mish, Michael. A Kid's Eye View of the Environment.

"Bats Eat Bugs." Banana Slug String Band. Adventures on the Air Cycle.

"Bats Eat Bugs." Miché, Mary. Nature Nuts.

"Brown Air." Banana Slug String Band. Dirt Made My Lunch.

"Bye Bye Dodo." Chapin, Tom. Billy the Squid.

"Don't Give My Green Shoes the Blues." (John Townsend and the Safe Swuad) Put on Your Green Shoes.

"Ecology." Banana Slug String Band. Adventures on the Air Cycle.

"Evergreen, Everblue." Raffi. Evergreen, Everblue.

"Evergreen, Everblue." Raffi. Raffi on Broadway.

"Garbage Blues." Tickle Tune Typhoon. Hug the Earth.

"Good Garbage." Chapin, Tom. Mother Earth.

"Green Grass Grew All Around." Seeger, Pete. Stories and Songs for Children.

"Green Grass Grows All Around." Roth, Kevin. Oscar, Bingo, and Buddies.

"Green Grass Grows All Around." Roth, Kevin. Travel Song Sing Alongs.

"Green Grass Grows All Around." Seeger, Pete. Abiyoyo and Other Story Songs for Children.

"Green Grass Grows All Around." Wee Sing Silly Songs.

"Green Shoes Walk." (Next Issue) Put on Your Green Shoes.

"Green Up." Shontz, Bill. Animal Tales.

"Hey, Hey, Don't Throw It Away." Miché, Mary. Nature Nuts.

"Hole in the Ozone." Shontz, Bill. Animal Tales.

"Just like the Sun." Raffi. Evergreen, Everblue.

"Just like the Sun." Raffi. Everything Grows.

"Keep It Green." Harley, Bill. Big Big World.

"The Light of the Sun." (Richie Havens and Rockapella) Put on Your Green Shoes.

"Our Oceans." Cappelli, Frank. Take a Seat!

"Pollution." Miché, Mary. Nature Nuts.

"Put on Your Green Shoes." (3 Cats 'n Jammers) Put on Your Green Shoes.

"Recycle Depot." Avni, Fran. Daisies and Ducklings.

"Recycle Rex." Craig 'n Co. Rock 'n Toontown.

"The Recycle Song." Rogers, Sally. Piggyback Planet.

"River." Cassidy, Nancy. Kids' Songs Sleepyheads.

"See the Beauty." Vitamin L. Everyone's Invited.

"Trash in the River." Mish, Michael. A Kid's Eye View of the Environment.

"Water." Lonnquist, Ken. Welcome 2 Kenland.

"We Recycle." The Van Manens. We Recycle.

"What Have They Done to the Rain?" Rogers, Sally. Piggyback Planet.

"What's the Matter with Us?" Raffi. Evergreen, Everblue.

"The Wheel of the Water." Chapin, Tom. Mother Earth.

"Who Made This Mess?" Harley, Bill. Big Big World.

"Who Made This Mess?" Pease, Tom. Wobbi-Do-Wop.

"Yecch!" Alsop, Peter. Wha'd'ya Wanna Do?

Emotions

"If You're Happy." Tickle Tune Typhoon. Hug the Earth.

This traditional song is very popular at children's parties and get-togethers. Some versions instruct you to perform a variety of actions only if you're happy. Tickle Tune Typhoon's version leads you through other emotions (happy, silly, sad, mad). Make up your own commands, the sillier the better. ("If you're grumpy and you know it, tickle your neighbor.") "If You're Happy" can also be found on:

Arnold, Linda. Happiness Cake.
Greg and Steve. We All Live Together, Vol. 3.
Little Richard. Shake It All About.
Marxer, Marcy. Jump Children.
Monet, Lisa. Circle Time.　　　　　　　　**(Ps, Pr)**

"I'm So Mad I Could Scream." Weissman, Jackie. Peanut Butter, Tarzan, and Roosters.

Not only does the singer get mad enough to scream and stomp, but also sad enough to cry and glad enough to sigh. Cover your ears as the kids make the noises associated with each emotion. Let them make up their own verses. *(Ps, Pr)*

"It's OK." Rosenshontz. Rosenshontz Tickles You.

Many songs and stories that address children's nighttime fears inadvertently give the children new fears to worry about. This song doesn't do that. This very reassuring song makes a good match for the picture book *Two Terrible Frights* by Jim Aylesworth. In the book, a little girl and a little mouse manage to scare each other. *(Ps, Pr)*

"Just Not Fair." Nagler, Eric. Improvise with Eric Nagler.

Nagler sings of all the injustices kids suffer at the hands of grown-ups (bathing more than once a year and wearing clean underwear). Play the recording and let the kids shout "It's just not fair!" at the appropriate times. Very funny. "Just Not Fair" was written by Nagler and Diana Buckley.

(Pr, I)

"Love Is a Special Way of Feeling." Avni, Fran. Artichokes and Brussel Sprouts.

Don't overlook this beautiful song written by Avni and sung by her and her daughter Ronit. It is one of the best children's love songs I've come across. *(All)*

"Mad at Me." (Dan Conley) Early Ears: Songs Just for 5 Year Olds.

The child in this song is frustrated because the parents always get mad about messy rooms, accidents, and fights with sister. Your children can join in on the chorus when the singer shouts "mad at me!" (as in "I hate it when you get . . ."). "Mad at Me" is performed by Dan Conley.

(Ps, Pr)

"Magic Penny." Tickle Tune Typhoon. Circle Around.

Love is like a magic penny. If you give it away, "you end up having more." Your audience will not be able to resist joining the wonderful chorus. This popular song was written by one of the best—Malvina Reynolds. "Magic Penny" can also be found on:

> Berman, Marcia. Marcia Berman Sings Malvina
>   Reynolds' Rabbit Dance.
> Fink, Cathy. When the Rain Comes Down.
> Fink, Cathy, and Marcy Marxer. A Cathy and Marcy
>   Collection for Kids.
> The Flyers. Family Hug.
> Tickle Tune Typhoon. Circle Around.   ***(All)***

"Show Me What You Feel." Greg and Steve. Kids in Motion.

Greg and Steve have designed an upbeat activity that allows children to act out their emotions. Show how you feel when you're happy, mad, excited, hungry, and so on. Use this song for theatrical warm-ups.   ***(All)***

"Skinnamarink." Sharon, Lois and Bram. One Elephant, Deux Elephants.

Sharon, Lois and Bram have made this traditional song one of their trademark themes. They use several hand motions to convey the emotion of love. Point to your eye for "I," point to your heart for "love," and point to the object of your affection for "you." Sometimes called "Skidamarink," it can also be found on:

> Cassidy, Nancy. Kids' Songs Sleepyheads.
> Gemini. Pulling Together.
> Marxer, Marcy. Jump Children.
> Sharon, Lois and Bram. The Elephant Show Record.
> Sharon, Lois and Bram. Great Big Hits.
> Sharon, Lois and Bram. One, Two, Three, Four, Live!
>   ***(Ps, Pr)***

"Smile." Wee Sing Sing-Alongs.

This traditional song is sung to "The Battle Hymn of the

Republic." "It isn't any trouble just to S-M-I-L-E." The formula is set for you to sing about other happy variations. "It isn't any trouble just to L-A-U-G-H" and "G-R-I-N Grin." The last verse has everyone singing "ha-ha-ha" throughout the whole tune. The accompanying booklet contains the entire set of lyrics. Guaranteed to bring out the smiles.

(All)

"State Laughs." Chapin, Tom. Moonboat.

Tennessee residents go hee-hee, Arkansas folks go haw-haw, and so on. Everyone gets to sing "and ro-ho-ho-ho-ho-ll on the floor." The group Vitamin L has a similar song in "Laughter" from their recording *Everyone's Invited*. They guffaw in Saginaw, tee-hee by the Isle of Capri, and more. Older kids might be able to add their own suggestions. "State Laughs" was written by John Forster. *(I)*

Here are more great songs about emotions:

"Add It Up." Bethie. Bethie's Really Silly Songs about Numbers.
"Boom Boom Boom." Arnold, Linda. Make Believe.
"Cheer Up." Penner, Fred. What a Day!
"Don't Whine." The Van Manens. Healthy Planet, Healthy People.
"Don't You Push Me Down." Guthrie, Woody. Woody's 20 Grow Big Songs.
"Faces." Block, Cathy. Timeless.
"Feeling Sorry." Troubadour. Can We Go Now?
"A Friend like You." Penner, Fred. What a Day!
"Happy Place." Rosenshontz. Share It.
"Happy to Be Here." Parachute Express. Happy to Be Here.
"Hey, We'll Fill the World with Love." Rosenshontz. Rosenshontz Tickles You.
"I Cried." Alsop, Peter. Stayin' Over.
"I Cried." Pelham, Ruth. Under One Sky.

"I Don't Believe It." Harley, Bill. You're in Trouble.

"I'm Angry." The Van Manens. We Recycle.

"I'm Bored." Craig 'n Co. Rock 'n Toontown.

"In My Heart." The Chenille Sisters. The Big Picture.

"I've Got the Blues, Greens and Reds." Chapin, Tom. Billy the Squid.

"Katy Don't Be Sad." The Flyers. Your Smile.

"A Laugh Can Turn It Around." The Chenille Sisters. 1-2-3 for Kids.

"Little Wheel A Turning." The Flyers. Your Smile.

"L.O.V.E." Arnold, Linda. Happiness Cake.

"Love Is a Little Word." Foote, Norman. If the Shoe Fits.

"Mikey Won't." Chapin, Tom. Zag Zig.

"Phobias." McCutcheon, John. Family Garden.

"Smile." LaFond, Lois. One World.

"Some Days Are Happier than Others." LaFond, Lois. One World.

"Sunny Side Up." Parachute Express. Sunny Side Up.

"Talk It Out." Pirtle, Sarah. Magical Earth.

"There's a Little Wheel A-Turning in My Heart." Sharon, Lois and Bram. The Elephant Show Record.

"There's Always Something You Can Do." Pirtle, Sarah. Two Hands Hold the Earth.

"Things Are Coming My Way." Pease, Tom. I'm Gonna Reach.

"Tommy Says." Harley, Bill. Big Big World.

"When You Smile." Bartels, Joanie. Jump for Joy.

"Where Are My Feelings." Fink, Cathy, and Marcy Marxer. Help Yourself.

"Wherever You Go, I Love You." Cassidy, Nancy. Kids' Songs Sleepyheads.

"Words." Tickle Tune Typhoon. Hearts and Hands.

"Yo Yo." Wozniak, Doug. Hugs and Kisses.

Family

"In My Family's House." O'Brien, Bruce. In My Family's House.

O'Brien presents a traditional pattern song based on the comforting things children find in their homes and with their families. "There'll be joy, joy, joy in my family's house. . . ." "There'll be lots of love in my family's house. . . " and so on. Ask the children what they like about their house. These contributions can either be serious or silly. There'll be chocolate chip cookies, lots of music, family hugs, Nintendo games. . . . **(All)**

"The Mother Song." Neat, Roxanne, and David Stoeri. Dance, Boatman, Dance.

Looking for a heartfelt Mother's Day gift? Try this song.

> *I've got a mother and you know that I'd druther*
> *not have any other mother but her.*
> *'Cause me and my brother and my sis and my brothers other*
> *we all love her lots.*

"The Mother Song" was written by David Stoeri. **(Pr, I)**

"My Aunt Came Back." Nagler, Eric. Fiddle Up a Tune.

This gyrating call-and-response favorite will have your audience screaming and moving in all directions. "My aunt came back from Timbuktu and brought with her a wooden shoe." The kids then stomp one foot. Add to that motion the actions of a waving fan, some pinking shears, a hula-hoop, and a rocking chair. Ask the children to think of new gifts their "aunt" can bring back and an accompanying motion. This song is a good closing activity for your session. Nagler has another gyrating song called "Big Green Monster" from *Come On In*. **(Pr, I)**

"My Dad." Charette, Rick. Where Do My Sneakers Go at Night?

Mercer Mayer's picture book *Just Me and My Dad* is a good companion to this song. Both the book and the song describe the pleasures of spending time with Dad (going on hikes, getting hugs, and more). Read the book, then play the tape. "My Dad" was written by Charette. ***(Ps, Pr)***

"Super Mom." Nagler, Eric. Improvise with Eric Nagler.

Nagler has created yet another frenzied movement song. He directs the children to wash windows with one hand, work the computer with the other hand, bounce the baby with their hips, and so on. Have the children think of all the busy activities their "Super Moms" do in one day. Add their suggestions to the song and everyone will be sure to become exhausted just trying to keep up with their "Super Moms." ***(Pr, I)***

"Why Did I Have to Have a Sister?" Diamond, Charlotte. 10 Carrot Diamond.

This song is popular in our house (one boy and three girls). It's a great match with Elaine Edleman's picture book *I Love My Baby Sister (Most of the Time)*. Diamond provides equal opportunity with a verse asking, "Why do I have to have a brother?" "Why Did I Have to Have a Sister?" was written by Diamond. ***(All)***

Here are more great songs about families:

"All of My Sisters Are Girls." Jennings, Waylon. Cowboys, Sisters, Rascals, and Dirt.

"Aunt Priscilla." Neat, Roxanne, and David Stoeri. The Bell Cow Swing.

"Be Kind to Your Parents." Arnold, Linda. Make Believe.

"Be Kind to Your Parents." Feinstein, Michael. Pure Imagination.

"Be Kind to Your Parents." Nagler, Eric. Come On In.

"Boogie Boogie Boogie." Pease, Tom. Boogie Boogie Boogie.

"Brothers and Sisters." Rosenshontz. Uh-Oh.

"Dad's Got That Look." McCutcheon, John. Family Garden.

"Daddy Be a Horsie." Palmer, Hap. Babysong.

"Daddy Does the Dishes." Rosenshontz. Family Vacation.

"Deva DeValita." (Taj Mahal) American Children.

"Don't Trick Your Dad." Alsop, Peter. Wha'd'ya Wanna Do?

"Families Are Made of Love." Atkinson, Lisa. The One and Only Me.

"Family." Craig 'n Co. Rock 'n Together.

"Family." Harley, Bill. You're in Trouble.

"Family Revival." McCutcheon, John. Family Garden.

"The Family Song." Tickle Tune Typhoon. Healthy Beginnings.

"The Family Song." Tickle Tune Typhoon. Hug the Earth.

"Family Tree." Chapin, Tom. Family Tree.

"Family Tree." (Tom Chapin) Rainbow Sign.

"Give Him Back." Rosen, Gary. Tot Rock.

"Goin' to Gramma and Grandpa's House." Kinnoin, David. Daring Dewey.

"Grandma." Pelham, Ruth. Under One Sky.

"Grandma's Patchwork Quilt." (Larry Penn) Grandma's Patchwork Quilt.

"Happy Adoption Day." McCutcheon, John. Family Garden.

"He's My Brother, She's My Sister." Bishop, Heather. Bellybutton.

"How Many People." McCutcheon, John. Family Garden.

"I Drive My Mommy Crazy." Rosen, Gary. Tot Rock.

"I Remember When." Brown, Greg. Bathtub Blues.

"It Takes Two to Make One." Rosenshontz. Rosenshontz Tickles You.

"It's My Family." McCutcheon, John. Family Garden.

"It's My Mother and My Father and My Sister and the Dog." Polisar, Barry Louis. Family Trip.

"Katy." Paxton, Tom. The Marvellous Toy.

"Logical." Alsop, Peter. Take Me with You.

"Mother's Day." Chapin, Tom. Moonboat.

"My Mother Ran Away Today." Polisar, Barry Louis. Family Concert.

"One Big Happy Family." Janet and Judy. Hotbilly Hits.

"Our Family." Arnold, Linda. Happiness Cake.

"Rock a Little, Baby." Cassidy, Nancy. Kids' Songs Sleepyheads.

"Rock a Little, Baby." Penner, Fred. Fred Penner's Place.

"Shine On." Kahn, Si. Good Times and Bed Times.

"The Sister Brother Song." Block, Cathy. Timeless.

"Two Kinds of Seagulls." Chapin, Tom. Mother Earth.

"What Does Your Mama Do?" Fink, Cathy. Grandma Slid down the Mountain.

"What Does Your Mama Do?" Pease, Tom. Boogie Boogie Boogie.

"What Does Your Mama Do?" Winter, Cathy, and Betsy Rose. As Strong as Anyone Can Be.

"Yesterday I Gave Away My Brother (Not Really)." Charette, Rick. Bubble Gum and Other Songs for Hungry Kids.

Farms

* "Cluck, Cluck, Red Hen." Raffi. Corner Grocery Store.

> Raffi sings a version of "Baa, Baa, Black Sheep" with new lyrics by Jacquelyn Reinach. Along with the black sheep, we hear "Cluck, cluck, red hen," "Moo, moo, brown cow," and "Buzz, buzz, busy bee." Sing the song while holding up pictures of a sheep, a hen, a cow, and a bee. Glue a "cheat sheet" of the lyrics on the back of the pictures. This allows you to read the words while the kids focus in on the pictures. "Cluck, Cluck, Red Hen" can also be found on:
> Cassidy, Nancy. Kids' Songs 2. **(Ps)**

"Cows Night Out." (Karan and the Musical Medicine Show)
Early Ears: Songs Just for 4 Year Olds.

When Farmer Jones closes up the barn for the night, he doesn't realize the cows are going to "cut the rug." *Barn Dance,* a picture book by Bill Martin, Jr., and John Archaumbault, is a perfect match for this song. In the book, the entire barnyard population starts dancing. "Cows Night Out" was written by Karan Bunin Huss. A similar tune is John McCutcheon's "Barnyard Dance" from his recording *Mail Myself to You.* In this song, the fruits and vegetables and crops dance late at night. **(Ps, Pr)**

* "Down on the Farm." Greg and Steve. We All Live Together, Vol. 5.

Kids make rooster, cow, pig, dog, horse, turkey, donkey, and people noises ("How do you do?") to the tune of "The Wheels on the Bus." This noisy song was written by Greg Scelsa. **(Ps, Pr)**

"Father Grumble." McCutcheon, John. Howjadoo.

A farmer tells his wife that he could do more work in one day than she could do in three. One disaster after another strikes him after they trade jobs in this traditional song. He soon realizes she does more work in one day than he does in seven! Play this recording after reading *The Man Who Kept House,* a Norwegian folk story told by P. C. Asbjornsen and J. E. Moe. The book is about a similar braggart with similar results. **(Pr)**

"Grandpa's Farm." Marxer, Marcy. Jump Children.

There are plenty of barnyard sound effects in this traditional song. "Down on Grandpa's farm there is a big, brown cow. The cow it goes a lot like this—Moo!" Have the children add their own verses. Instruct them to shout out an animal and a color (real or silly) to go with the animal. For more fun, have them think of animals not typically found on farms. "Down on Grandpa's farm there is a black and white zebra." Try inanimate objects, too. "Down on Grandpa's farm there is a bright, green tractor." "Mi chacra," from *Wee Sing around the World* and "Welcome to My Farm" from Bonnie Phipps's *Monsters' Holiday* are Spanish versions of the song. Other versions of "Grandpa's Farm" can be found on:

> Fink, Cathy, and Marcy Marxer. A Cathy and Marcy
>   Collection for Kids.
> Raffi. One Light, One Sun.
> Sharon, Lois and Bram. All the Fun You Can Sing!
> Sharon, Lois and Bram. Great Big Hits.
> Sharon, Lois and Bram. Sing A to Z.   ***(Ps)***

"Hard Scrabble Harvest." Herdman, Priscilla. Daydreamer.

Herdman added the music to the text of the Dahlov Ipcar picture book of the same name. A farmer goes through a lot of hard work to raise his crops. There are horses to chase out of the melons, 'coons in the corn, crows in the pea patch, rabbits, deer, and the frost—whew! And then, after all that work, the relatives gobble up what's left!   ***(All)***

"Heading On Down to the Barn." Grammer, Red. Down the Do-Re-Mi.

Kathy and Red Grammer wrote this song about animals in a barn who were happy to see the singers coming. The singers knew this was true because

> *The cat meowed*
> *and the dog went "Woof"*
> *and the horse went "Neigh"*
> *and stomped his hoof*
> *and the turkey gobble-gobbled*
> *and the cow went "Moo"*
> *and the itty-bitty baby went "Boo-hoo-hoo"*
> *'cause he was hungry, too.*

Write out these chorus lyrics so your kids can join the children on the recording.   ***(All)***

"Many Cows." Pease, Tom. Boogie Boogie Boogie.

In Wisconsin, where Pease lives and where songwriter Anna Lee Scully spent some time, there are many, many cows.

Listen to Pease rhapsodize about the wonders of cows. The kids can echo him singing "many, many, many, many, many, many cows." And it wouldn't be a good cow song if there weren't ample chances for the kids to "Moo!" **(All)**

"Oats and Beans and Barley." Raffi. Baby Beluga.

Kids can act out the farmer's motions during this traditional, circle-dance song. Start the kids miming the planting of the seeds and watering the ground, then stamping their feet, clapping their hands, and turning around to view the land. A similar version can be found on:
> Gemini. Pulling Together.
> Wee Sing and Play.   **(Ps, Pr)**

* "Old MacDonald Had a 'Whzz.'" Weissman, Jackie. Peanut Butter, Tarzan, and Roosters.

Weissman doesn't use farm animals in her variation of the popular, traditional song. Instead, she uses mouthsounds (tongue clicks, lip blurbles, raspberries, coughs, and sneezes). Other variations of "Old MacDonald" include:
> "The Old MacDonald Swing." Janet and Judy. Hotbilly Hits.
> "Rock and Roll MacDonald." Scruggs, Joe. Deep in the Jungle.

For those looking for more traditional versions, listen to:
> Little Richard. Shake It All About.
> Roth, Kevin. Oscar, Bingo, and Buddies.
> Wee Sing.   **(Ps, Pr)**

"On the Funny Farm." Rosenshontz. Uh-Oh.

On this farm, the dog goes meow, the horse goes cluck, and the owl goes hee-haw. The picture book *Down on the Funny Farm* by P. E. King has similar mixed-up critters. Read the book, then listen to Rosenshontz. Or listen to Linda Arnold's song "Barnyard Talk" from her recording *Happiness Cake*. Her song is about a purple cow that clucks and lays a purple egg. "On the Funny Farm" was written by Gary Rosen, Bill Shontz, and George Storey.   **(Ps, Pr)**

"The Planting Song." Buckner, Janice. Little Friends for Little Folks.

This cumulative song covers the stages of planting the crops in the fields. From getting on the tractor to hooking up the plow and turning the soil to throwing the seed and praying for rain, this instructional (yet fun) song will help children appreciate all the work it takes to grow crops. "The Planting Song" was written by Buckner. **(Ps, Pr)**

"When I First Came to This Land." Diamond, Charlotte. Diamond in the Rough.

Starting a farm from scratch is a lot of hard work. The singer calls her horse "trouble, of course," her cow "no milk now," her shack "break my back," and her farm "muscle in my arm." This cumulative, traditional song is not too difficult to learn. Add some motions to the words, such as holding your back as if in pain for "break by back," making milking motions for "no milk now," and making a muscle for "muscle in my arm." Have the children make up motions for the other animals mentioned in the song. This is a good song for a class to rehearse and perform for an assembly. "When I First Came to This Land" can also be found on:
>Harley, Bill. 50 Ways to Fool Your Mother.
>Rosenthal, Phil. The Paw Paw Patch.   **(All)**

Here are more great songs about farms:

"The Ballad of Reuben Rooster." Crow, Dan. Oops!

"The Barn Dance." Bishop, Heather. Bellybutton.

"Barnyard Boogie." Grammer, Red. Teaching Peace.

"The Bellcow." Nagler, Eric. Improvise with Eric Nagler.

"Chickens on Vacation." Charette, Rick. Chickens on Vacation.

"Chickery Chick." Marxer, Marcy. Jump Children.

"Cluck Old Hen." Nagler, Eric. Improvise with Eric Nagler.

"Down on the Farm." Parachute Express. Circle of Friends.

"The Farmer in the Dell." Wee Sing and Play.

"The Farmer's Market." Abell, Timmy. The Farmer's Market.

"Go'n to Gramma's Farm." Wozniak, Doug. Hugs and Kisses.

"Heavenly Music." Greg and Steve. Playing Favorites.

"Hinky Dinky 'Double D' Farm." Wee Sing Silly Songs.

"Little Rooster." Grunsky, Jack. Waves of Wonder.

"Miranda Was Born in a Barn." Crow, Dan. Oops!

"The Seed Cycle." Wee Sing and Play.

"Sittin' on a Farm." Bethie. Bethie's Really Silly Songs about Animals.

"There Ain't Nobody Here but Us Chickens." Nagler, Eric. Improvise with Eric Nagler.

"There Ain't Nobody Here but Us Chickens." Pease, Tom. Boogie Boogie Boogie.

Food

"10 Crunchy Carrots." Diamond, Charlotte. 10 Carrot Diamond.

My friend Colleen heard about using felt carrots with this song and passed the idea on to me. Make ten felt carrots and line them up on a felt board. Make one carrot with two halves. Several carrot patterns can be found in *Felt Board Fun* by Liz and Dick Wilmes. One by one, the carrots are eaten by sisters, bees, worms, Dracula, gerbils, and other hungry creatures. The last carrot is "broken in two" to share "a piece for me and a piece for you." "10 Crunchy Carrots" was written by Diamond. ***(Ps, Pr)***

"Corner Grocery Store." Raffi. Corner Grocery Store.

Imagine cheese walking on its knees, plums twiddling their thumbs, corn blowing a horn, or beans trying on jeans. Ask the children to make up their own nonsensical food rhymes, such as "There was stew, stew, putting on a shoe." Have someone draw pictures of these images on a chalkboard. It doesn't matter if the person is a good artist or not, especially with these silly visions. Better yet, draw them on posterboard and preserve them for your next crop of kids. This traditional song provides a good exercise in imaginative writing for older kids. *(All)*

* **"Cupcakes Just for Me." Peanutbutterjam. Peanutbutterjam Goes to School.**

There are ten cupcakes on the kitchen shelf. One by one they are taken by a bullfrog, dinosaur, elephant, spider, hummingbird, dragon, goldfish, kangaroo, and a monster. You could easily change the animals in this pattern song by Eileen Packard to fit any props that you have handy, such as puppets, pictures, or dolls. You can also make felt creations for this backwards counting song. *Felt Board Fun* by Liz and Dick Wilmes has a cupcake pattern. *(Ps, Pr)*

"I Am a Pizza." Diamond, Charlotte. 10 Carrot Diamond.

Peter Alsop wrote this popular call-and-response song about the many ingredients of pizza.

> *I am a pizza (I am a pizza)*
> *with extra cheese (with extra cheese).*
> *From tomatoes (from tomatoes)*
> *sauce is squeezed (sauce is squeezed).*
> *Garlic and mushrooms (garlic and mushrooms),*
> *oregano (oregano),*
> *I am a pizza ready to go.*

Diamond's version contains a verse sung in French. "I Am a Pizza" can also be found on:
Alsop, Peter. Wha'd'ya Wanna Do?
Arnold, Linda. Peppermint Wings. *(All)*

"I'm a Little Cookie." (Larry Penn) Grandma's Patchwork Quilt.

Composer Larry Penn sings his original song, which sounds like it's about food, but is really about self-esteem and handicaps. On this version, he gives a wonderful introduction on how the song was created. Try making felt pieces of the food he sings about (two halves of a cookie, a Tootsie Roll with a twist, a bent chocolate bar, and a gumdrop with a dent). "I'm a Little Cookie" can also be found on:

McCutcheon, John. Mail Myself to You.

Pease, Tom. Boogie Boogie Boogie.

Phipps, Bonnie. Monsters' Holiday.   **(All)**

"Jelly, Jelly in My Belly." Sharon, Lois and Bram. The Elephant Show Record.

Your children's imaginations will make or break this cumulative song. "2-4-6-8, tell me what is on your plate!" Sharon, Lois and Bram respond with hamburgers, bagels, butterscotch sundaes, liver and spinach, and brownies. The added challenge is reciting everything backwards during each chorus.   **(Pr, I)**

"Lima Beans and Diced Beets." Rappin' Rob. The Rappin' Rob Rap.

This variation of the traditional "Apples and Bananas" features Rappin' Rob's two favorite foods. Change the vowels of the song and instead of singing "I like to eat, eat, eat lima beans and diced beets," the kids will be singing phrases like "I like to oat, oat, oat lomo bones and doced boats." Tom Pease adds verses doctoring the phrase "pepperoni pizza" on his version of "Apples and Bananas," from *Boogie Boogie Boogie*. Traditional versions of "Apples and Bananas" can be found on:

Cassidy, Nancy. Kids' Songs.

Crow, Dan. Oops!

Raffi. One Light, One Sun.

Raffi. Raffi in Concert with the Rise and Shine Band.

                    (Pr, I)

"Meatballs and Spaghetti." Phipps, Bonnie. Dinosaur Choir.

Phipps asks several questions to which the answer is always "meatballs and spaghetti." Kids will not only have fun shouting out this answer, but also thinking of new questions. My suggestions include "What do you serve the president? Meatballs and spaghetti!" and "What is your baby brother's name? Meatballs and spaghetti!" *(All)*

"The Ooh Ooh Song." Block, Cathy. Timeless.

Block introduces her cinnamon juice, onion perfume, and vegetable cake. The reaction is always the same—"ooh ooh ooh ooh" (as in "ooh yuk"). Block implores everyone to try them, but doesn't get any takers by the end of her original song. *(All)*

"Peanutbutter." Peanutbutterjam. Incredibly Spreadable.

The children on the tape throw out suggestions of what they like with their "peanutbutterjam." Their creative ideas include peanutbutter cookies, peanutbutter ice cream, peanutbutter snakes, and peanutbutter sneakers. All of the kids clap whenever the word "jam" is sung. This pattern song, created as an ode to the duo Peanutbutterjam, was written by group member Eileen Packard. *(Ps, Pr)*

"Recipe." Troubadour. Can We Go Now?

This chocolate chip cookie recipe song includes licking the bowl, the spoon, the sugar, and the batter. *The Doorbell Rang,* a picture book by Pat Hutchins, also features cookies. Share the song and the book with a plate of real chocolate chip cookies. "Recipe" was written by Victor Cockburn and Judith Steinbergh. *(Ps, Pr)*

"Still Hungry." Bethie. Bethie's Really Silly Songs about Numbers.

Bethie combines food with counting. She eats one cookie, two cherries, three pancakes, four raisins, five bananas, six enchiladas, seven peas, eight pickles, nine hot dogs, and ten chocolate cakes. This makes for a fun felt project (if you have enough felt and can make felt enchiladas). The children will have fun singing "I was sti-l-l-l HUNGRY!" *(All)*

"Stone Soup." Chapin, Tom. Mother Earth.

Read Marcia Brown's picture book *Stone Soup*. Chapin's song, written by Chapin and John Forster, is based on the same folktale. "The Wonderful Soup Stone" sung by Cowboy Steff from *The Giving Tree and Other Shel Silverstein Songs* doesn't follow the same story, but lists ridiculous ingredients to add to the soup (crocodile bones, mudpies, frogs wearing bow ties, and more).   *(All)*

"The Vegetable Lament." Arnold, Linda. Make Believe.

Vegetables get to tell their side of the story. They have low self-esteem because they heard kids shout how they hate vegetables. Create felt beets, spinach, broccoli, cauliflower, and carrots. Many of these patterns can be found in the Wilmes's *Felt Board Fun*. Another fine vegetable song is "V-E-G-E-T-A-B-L-E-S," written and performed by Doug Wozniak from *Music for Miles of Smiles*. Wozniak has children hold up cards of all of the letters in "Vegetables" as he spells it out. This funny song is all about the trials of getting a child to eat his V-E-G-E-T-A-B-L-E-S.   *(Pr)*

"Watermelon." McCutcheon, John. Family Garden.

McCutcheon wrote this hilarious song as part of a song-writing workshop with six- and seven-year-olds. The chorus is full of sound effects such as slurping, spitting "the seeds," and going "ahhh." Play the recording and act out eating a big slice of juicy watermelon.   *(Pr, I)*

Here are more great songs about food:

"Aiken Drum." Carfra, Pat. Songs for Sleepyheads and Out-of-Beds.

"Aikendrum." Raffi. Singable Songs for the Very Young.

"The Ballad of Lucy Lumm." Phipps, Bonnie. Monsters' Holiday.

"Bananas." Rosenshontz. It's the Truth.

"Biscuits in the Oven." Raffi. Baby Beluga.

"Bubblegum." Peanutbutterjam. Incredibly Spreadable.

"Chew Chew Cha Cha." Tickle Tune Typhoon. Healthy Beginnings.

"Chicken Lips and Lizard Hips." Cassidy, Nancy. Kids' Songs.

"Cookies." Fink, Cathy. When the Rain Comes Down.

"Cooking Breakfast for the Ones I Love." Muldaur, Maria. On the Sunny Side.

"Eat It Up." Rosenshontz. Share It.

"Food for Thought." Craig 'n Co. Rock 'n Toontown.

"The Fruit Song." The Chenille Sisters. The Big Picture.

"Gobble Gobble Munch." Drake, David HB. Kid-Stuff.

"Going on a Picnic." Raffi. Corner Grocery Store.

"It's No Fun When Ya Gotta Eat an Onion." Alsop, Peter. Take Me with You.

"It's So Good." Janet and Judy. Hotbilly Hits.

"Mashed Potatoes." Paxton, Tom. Peanut Butter Pie.

"Mrs. Murphy's Chowder." Cassidy, Nancy. Kids' Songs 2.

"Mrs. Murphy's Chowder." Phipps, Bonnie. Dinosaur Choir.

"Pancakes." Pease, Tom. Wobbi-Do-Wop.

"Pasta." Arnold, Linda. Peppermint Wings.

"P.B. and J." Craig 'n Co. Morning 'n Night.

"Peanut Butter." McCutcheon, John. Howjadoo.

"Peanut Butter." Parachute Express. Shakin' It!

"Peanut Butter." Sharon, Lois and Bram. Smorgasbord.

"Peanut Butter Pie." Paxton, Tom. Peanut Butter Pie.

"Pizza Shake." Harley, Bill. Big Big World.

"The Popcorn Pop." Rosen, Gary. Tot Rock.

"Sandwiches." Alsop, Peter. Wha'd'ya Wanna Do?

"Sandwiches." Cassidy, Nancy. Kids' Songs 2.

"Sandwiches." Penner, Fred. The Cat Came Back.

"Sandwiches." Penner, Fred. Collections.

"Sitting in the Soup." Pirtle, Sarah. The Wind Is Telling Secrets.

"Smorgasbord." Sharon, Lois and Bram. Smorgasbord.

"The Three Foot Sandwich." Phipps, Bonnie. Monsters' Holiday.

"Trading Lunches." Marin, Cheech. My Name Is Cheech, the School Bus Driver.

"You Gotta Have a Peanut Butter Song." Kahn, Si. Good Times and Bed Times.

Friendship

"The ABC's of You." Grammer, Red. Down the Do-Re-Mi.

Grammer offers a litany of complimentary adjectives from "A-1 grade A" to "One in a zillion." Grammer sings the first verse, his son David sings it a second time, and they both trade lines the third time through. "The ABC's of You" was written by Red and Kathy Grammer. It can also be found on:

Penner, Fred. What a Day!

The song is similar to the classic "A, You're Adorable" which can be found on:

Sharon, Lois and Bram. Great Big Hits.
Sharon, Lois and Bram. Smorgasbord.   *(Pr, I)*

"Circle of Friends." Parachute Express. Circle of Friends.

Parachute Express is a fun trio who specialize in unique harmonies and creative arrangements. Here, they encourage everyone to get into a friendship circle, move to the left, move to the right, move forward, then backward. The clapping people on the recording sound like they are having lots of fun, as will your kids. Another fun friendship circle song is Malvina Reynolds's "Move Over," in which friends crowd into a circle and invite more friends to join them. "Move Over" can be found on:

Berman, Marcia. Marcia Berman Sings Malvina
   Reynolds' Rabbits Dance.
Sharon, Lois and Bram. All the Fun You Can Sing!
Sharon, Lois and Bram. Mainly Mother Goose.   *(All)*

"The Crow's Toes." Paxton, Tom. Suzy Is a Rocker.

The chorus is simple. You are the crow's toes, flea's cheese, ant's pants, and bee's knees (which are indeed complimentary). Have the children create more silly rhymes for this quiet song. "The Crow's Toes" was written by Paxton.

(Pr, I)

* "Friends Are Special." Cassidy, Nancy. Kids' Songs Sleepyheads.

"Friends are special when they sing together. They can sing the whole day. They can sing the night away. They can sing together. They can sing." Replace the word "sing" in this traditional pattern song with "laugh," "cry," "dream," and whatever else the children can suggest. *(All)*

"Justin." Scruggs, Joe. Abracadabra.

It's a sad time when a friend moves away. Justin has been the narrator's friend since they were both three years old. Now Justin has to move because his mom's new job is in another town. The narrator cries all day and night. Another moving song is Joanie Bartels's "Why Does It Hurt So Much?" Both songs are good matches for Bernard Waber's picture book *Ira Says Goodbye*. *(Ps, Pr)*

* "Won't You Be My Partner." O'Brien, Bruce. In My Family's House.

Won't you be my partner to walk in the woods,
Won't you be my partner to walk in the woods,
Won't you be my partner to walk in the woods,
I am brave and you are brave and I'm brave, too.

O'Brien also asks, "Won't you be my partner," to climb a hill, camp in a tent, sing by the fire, and meet new friends. Have the children add their own lyrics to this zipper song. "Won't You Be My Partner" was written by O'Brien's daughter Emma when she was three years old! *(All)*

Here are more great songs about friendship:

"Across the Wide Ocean." Pirtle, Sarah. Two Hands Hold the Earth.

"All of My Friends." Chapin, Tom. Billy the Squid.

"Best Friends." Phipps, Bonnie. Monsters' Holiday.

"Best of Friends." Dallas, Patti, and Laura Baron. Playtime Parade.

"Do It Together." Harley, Bill. Big Big World.

"A Friend like You." Penner, Fred. What a Day!

"Friend to You." (Dan Conley) Early Ears: Songs Just for 4 Year Olds.

"Friends." Livingston, Bob. Open the Window.

"Friends." Sprout, Jonathan. On the Radio.

"Friends Forever." Greg and Steve. We All Live Together, Vol. 5.

"Friendship Chain." Parachute Express. Happy to Be Here.

"Friendship Pin." Nagler, Eric. Come On In.

"A Good Friend." Rosenshontz. It's the Truth.

"Good Morning, Neighbors." Parachute Express. Circle of Friends.

"Handy Dandy." Craig 'n Co. Rock 'n Together.

"Hi Hi, I Love Ya." Chapin, Tom. Zag Zig.

"I Like You." Parachute Express. Feel the Music.

"I Made Myself a New Friend." Vitamin L. Singin' in the Key of L.

"I Want to Get to Know You." Vitamin L. Walk a Mile.

"Let's Be Friends." Tickle Tune Typhoon. All of Us Will Shine.

"Make New Friends." Sweet Honey in the Rock. All for Freedom.

"Make New Friends." Wee Sing Sing-Alongs.

"My Best Friend." Monet, Lisa. My Best Friend.

"Share It." Rosenshontz. Share It.

"That's What Friends Are For." Harley, Bill. Monsters in the Bathroom.

"Welcome." Vitamin L. Everyone's Invited.

"When You Come Over to My House." Parachute Express. Circle of Friends.

"With People I Like." Banana Slug String Band. Dirt Made My Lunch.

"You Must Really Like Me." Parachute Express. Shakin' It!

Frogs

"Five Little Frogs." Raffi. Singable Songs for the Very Young.

Five green and speckled frogs sit on a speckled log and jump into the pool one by one. Counting-backwards songs like this are perfect for felt board presentations. Make five felt frogs and a felt log. There is a good frog felt pattern in Judy Sierra's *The Flannel Board Storytelling Book*. Play the recording or sing it yourself as you remove the frog pieces one by one. Kids can shout "yum, yum" after Raffi sings about eating bugs. They can also make frog noises after each stanza. "Five Little Frogs" was written by Lucille Wood and Louise Scott. A similar version can be found on:

Quackity Yakity Bop. **(Ps)**

"The Foolish Frog." Seeger, Pete. Stories and Songs for Little Children.

Seeger's popular narrative is full of audience participation and sound effects. Play the recording and the children will soon start singing the infectious chorus. The kids who can't pick up the words to the chorus can join in with cow, chicken, and babbling brook noises. As the foolish frog swells up with pride, inflate a green balloon and pop it at the appropriate point. "The Foolish Frog" can also be found on:

Diamond, Charlotte. Diamond in the Rough. **(All)**

"Metamorphosis." Diamond, Charlotte. Diamond
in the Rough.

> "Metamorphosis" is a perfect match for Jack Kent's wonderful picture book *The Caterpillar and the Polliwog*. Folkmanis Puppets has two puppets—a caterpillar that turns into a butterfly and a tadpole that turns into a frog—that liven up both the enjoyment of the book and the recording. Beg a local service organization, PTA, or Friends of the Library group to purchase these puppets for you.
>
> *(Ps, Pr)*

"Newts, Salamanders, and Frogs." Banana Slug String Band.
Dirt Made My Lunch.

> Life getting you down? Then learn the pleasures of being an amphibian. The kids can sing "Oh yeah!" after each verse. This is one of those tunes that will rattle around in your head long after you've heard it (a "head hummer"). "Newts, Salamanders, and Frogs" was written by Steve Van Zandt and can also be found on:
> Miché, Mary. Nature Nuts. *(Pr, I)*

"The Night the Froggies Flew." Colleen and Uncle Squaty.
Colleen and Uncle Squaty.

> Frogs flying on lily pads make this song a perfect match for Dave Wiesner's picture book *Tuesday*. Hold up this wordless Caldecott Award winner while listening to Uncle Squaty sing. "The Night the Froggies Flew" was written by Brian Schellinger and Colleen Hannafin. *(All)*

"Twenty Froggies Went to School." Rosenthal, Phil.
Chickens in the Garden.

> This traditional folk song follows nearly the same text as Kate Duke's picture book *Seven Froggies Went to School*. Master Bullfrog teaches the young froggies to beware of cats, birds, muskrats, and—most of all—boys with sticks. Duke credits the words to George Cooper. *(Ps, Pr)*

Frogs

Here are more great songs about frogs:

"Blue Frog." Penner, Fred. What a Day!

"The Frog in the Bog." Wee Sing Fun 'n' Folk.

"Frog on the Log." Gibson, Dee, and Joe Scruggs. Songs to Brighten Your Day.

"Frog Went A-Courtin'." Seeger, Mike and Peggy. American Folk Songs for Children.

"Frog Went A-Courtin'." Seeger, Pete. Stories and Songs for Little Children.

"A Frog Went A-Courtin'." Wee Sing Fun 'n' Folk.

"Froggy Went A-Courtin'." Watson, Doc. Doc Watson Sings Songs for Little Pickers.

"Frogs in the Road." Charette, Rick. Bubble Gum and Other Songs for Hungry Kids.

"The Frog's Party." Walker, Mary Lu. The Frog's Party.

"The Garden (Frog and Toad)." Roth, Kevin. Unbearable Bears.

"Gat Goon." Sharon, Lois and Bram. All the Fun You Can Sing!

"Gatgoon." Sharon, Lois and Bram. Sing A to Z.

"Green Frogs." Carfra, Pat. Babes, Beasts, and Birds.

"Hippity Hop." Avni, Fran. Artichokes and Brussel Sprouts.

"Hop-a-Long Froggity." Wozniak, Doug. Music for Miles of Smiles.

"Keemo Kymo." Wee Sing Fun 'n' Folk.

"Kiddy Kum Kimo." Sharon, Lois and Bram. Sing A to Z.

"Mr. Froggie Went A-Courtin'." Ives, Burl. Little White Duck.

"Mister Froggy." Livingston, Bob. Open the Window.

"One Day My Best Friend Barbara Turned into a Frog." Polisar, Barry Louis. Old Dog, New Tricks.

"Peepers." Walker, Mary Lu. The Frog's Party.

"The Puffed Up Frog." Roth, Kevin. The Secret Journey.

"There Was an Old Frog." The Seeger Family. Animal Folk Songs for Children.

"Wish Me a Lot of Muck." Kinnoin, Dave. Dunce Cap Kelly.

Gardens

"Dirt Made My Lunch." Banana Slug String Band. Dirt Made My Lunch.

It's catchy. It's simple. It's an ode to dirt. Written by Steve Van Zandt. 'Nuff said. It can also be found on:
Miché, Mary. Earthy Tunes. **(All)**

"Family Garden." McCutcheon, John. Family Garden.

Play this song after reading Lois Ehlert's picture book, *Eating the Alphabet*. Both the song and book name specific vegetables, such as Japanese kale, pinto beans, and turnip greens. The song describes the steps involved in gardening (turning the soil, laying down the mulch, pulling weeds). "Family Garden" is peaceful, meditative, and written by McCutcheon and Si Kahn. **(Pr, I)**

"The Garden (Frog and Toad)." Roth, Kevin. Unbearable Bears.

Roth adapted Arnold Lobel's story from the book *Frog and Toad Together* into a wonderful song. Toad plants some seeds and impatiently yells at them to grow. Frog wisely teaches him to leave them alone. Read the book, then play the recording. **(Ps, Pr)**

"The Garden Song." Peter, Paul and Mary. Peter, Paul and Mommy, Too.

"Inch by inch, row by row . . ." begins the chorus of the prettiest garden song ever written. The children will quickly learn the chorus and join in. "The Garden Song" was written by David Mallet. It can also be found on:
A Child's Celebration of Song. (Maria Muldaur)
Diamond, Charlotte. 10 Carrot Diamond.
Family Folk Festival. (Maria Muldaur)
McCornack, Mike and Carleen. Sunshine Cake.
Miché, Mary. Earthy Tunes.
Rosenshontz. Rosenshontz Tickles You. **(All)**

"Oh, John the Rabbit." Seeger, Mike and Peggy. American Folk Songs for Children.

John the Rabbit has a mighty habit of jumping into the garden in this traditional song. Once there, he'll "cut down" the cabbage, sweet potatoes, and tomatoes. Kids can sing "Yes, ma'am" after each line. They can also insert their own garden items in the recital. Variations of "Oh, John the Rabbit" can be found on:

> Carfra, Pat. Lullabies and Laughter with the Lullaby Lady.
> Sharon, Lois and Bram. Mainly Mother Goose.　　*(All)*

"Zucchini Song." Crow, Dan. A Friend, a Laugh, a Walk in the Woods.

Anyone who has grown zucchini knows that you can soon have more than you can eat or give away. Dan Crow has a garden that has zucchini and carrots and zucchini and peas and zucchini and berries and zucchini and broccoli and zucchini and spiders and zucchini. The kids can shout "We have a garden!" during the chorus.　　*(Pr, I)*

Here are more great songs about gardens:

"The Changing Garden of Mister Bell." Parachute Express. Happy to Be Here.

"The Closet Key." Seeger, Mike and Peggy. American Folk Songs for Children.

"Going to My Garden." The Van Manens. We Recycle.

"In My Garden." Raffi. One Light, One Sun.

"Little Seed." Guthrie, Woody. Woody's 20 Grow Big Songs.

"The Magic Garden." The Chenille Sisters. The Big Picture.

"The Pumpkin Man." (John McCutcheon) Grandma's Patchwork Quilt.

"The Pumpkin Song." Peanutbutterjam. Peanutbutterjam Goes to School.

"Pumpkin Song." Walker, Mary Lu. The Frog's Party.

"Tulips and Daisies." Avni, Fran. Daisies and Ducklings.

"Yam Jam." Arnold, Linda. Peppermint Wings.

Growing Up

"Growing Song." Atkinson, Lisa. I Wanna Tickle the Fish.

> Atkinson sings about the honest feelings children have when they are impatient to grow up. The second half of the song turns into a round to the tune of "Row, Row, Row Your Boat." The kids slowly stand as they sing "children get taller" and slowly kneel when they sing "grownups get smaller." "Growing Song" was written by Atkinson. **(Pr)**

"I Wonder If I'm Growing." Raffi. Singable Songs for the Very Young.

> This Raffi original celebrates reaching the sink for the first time. The picture book *Happy Birthday, Sam* by Pat Hutchins is a wonderful match. Sam also celebrates memorable firsts, such as reaching the sink, the light switch, and the doorknob. **(Ps)**

"I'm Little." Jennings, Waylon. Cowboys, Sisters, Rascals, and Dirt.

> Jennings wrote this humorous song and does a nice job of describing the feelings of a small child wanting to grow up. The kids can echo the "I'm little" chorus. Jennings wrote a nice companion song called "I Just Can't Wait" on the same recording. **(Ps, Pr)**

* "I'm Not Small." Harley, Bill. Monsters in the Bathroom.

> Marcia Berman wrote this song of self-esteem. The children sing that they are not small. In fact, they are tall enough to carry a whale on their back. Have the children decide what heavy object they would like to pretend to carry on their backs (trucks, schools, libraries). "I'm Not Small" can also

be found on:
>Sharon, Lois and Bram. One Elephant, Deux Elephants.
>
>**(Ps)**

"Puff (The Magic Dragon)." Peter, Paul and Mary. Peter, Paul and Mommy.

Puff is no doubt the most famous dragon, and this song is arguably the best-known modern-day children's song. I've listed it under Growing Up, but it could easily fit under the Friendship or Imagination categories. Play the recording at a family event and all of the adults and most of the children will automatically start singing the chorus. Be sure to listen to young Amber McInnes's version on *Family Folk Festival*. It is especially moving. "Puff (The Magic Dragon)" was written by Peter Yarrow and Leonard Lipton and can also be found on:
>Arnold, Linda. Happiness Cake.
>Cassidy, Nancy. Kids' Songs.
>A Child's Celebration of Song. (Peter, Paul and Mary)
>Miché, Mary. Animal Crackers.
>Peter, Paul and Mary. Peter, Paul and Mommy, Too.
>Reggae for Kids. (Gregory Isaacs)
>Roth, Kevin. Dinosaurs, Dragons, and Other Children's
>>Songs.
>Roth, Kevin. Travel Song Sing Alongs.
>Sharon, Lois and Bram. Happy Birthday.
>
>**(All)**

"When I Was a Baby." Carfra, Pat. Songs for Sleepyheads and Out-of-Beds.

Carfra describes what a baby says ("wha-wha"), what a one-year-old says ("ma ma, da da"), and what a two-year-old says ("No! No!"). Ask the children what a three-, four-, or five-year-old would say. Better yet, use this song at a Family Storytime and ask the parents. They're the ones who know best.
>**(All)**

Here are more great songs about growing up:

"Because We're Kids." Feinstein, Michael. Pure Imagination.

"Big Boy." Craig 'n Co. Morning 'n Night.

"Bigger, Bigger, Bigger." Alsop, Peter. Stayin' Over.

"Everything Grows." Raffi. Everything Grows.

"Everything Grows." Raffi. Raffi on Broadway.

"Help Yourself." Fink, Cathy, and Marcy Marxer. Help Yourself.

"I Must Be Growing." Bennett, Glenn. I Must Be Growing.

"I Must Be Growing." (Glenn Bennett) Early Ears: Songs Just for 4 Year Olds.

"My Daddy Do Too." (Dan Conley) Early Ears: Songs Just for 2 Year Olds.

"Turn Around." Carfra, Pat. Lullabies and Laughter with the Lullaby Lady.

"Turn Around." Cassidy, Nancy. Kids' Songs Sleepyheads.

"Turn Around." McCutcheon, John. Mail Myself to You.

"Turn Around." Sharon, Lois and Bram. Happy Birthday.

"Younger Kid Stuff." Craig 'n Co. Rock 'n Toontown.

Imagination

"Abazaba Scooby Dooby." Arnold, Linda. Happiness Cake.

A goblin teaches a girl to say "Abazaba scooby dooby apa choka maka yeah" whenever she gets into trouble. Children love to learn phrases like this (remember "Supercalifragilisticexpialodocious"?). Teach it to the children before playing the recording. Then listen as the girl uses the phrase to escape a rhino, a giant, and a pterodactyl. "Abazaba Scooby Dooby" was written by Arnold. A similar song is "Goo Goo Ga Ga" by Joe Scruggs from his recording *Traffic Jams*. In Scruggs's song, a baby saves the day from a troll, a witch, and an alligator by singing "Goo goo ga ga and coochie coochie coo." **(Ps, Pr)**

"Computer Man." Schneider, Bob. When You Dream a Dream.

It will be hard to keep the children from moving like a

robot when they listen to this hypnotic, techno-pop music. There are several funny bits when the kids ask "Computer Man" some tough questions. Example: "How do you spell 'Supercalifragilisticexpialodocious'?" Answer: "With letters." "Computer Man" was written by Schneider. *(Pr, I)*

"A Fairy Went A-Marketing." Herdman, Priscilla. Daydreamer.

A fairy buys a fish, a bird, and a mouse, marvels at their beauty, and lets them go free. Play Herdman's recording after reading the picture book of the same title written by Rose Fyleman in 1918. Herdman wrote the music. *(Ps)*

"I Wish I Was." Rosenshontz. Rosenshontz Tickles You.

Kids will have fun throwing out suggestions for this zipper song. Have them name an animal they wish they could be. Then have them think of an action that rhymes with that animal. "I wish I was a mouse. I'd sleep inside your house." Rosenshontz includes rhymes for dogs, gorillas, ostriches, monkeys, bears, and camels. Wait until you hear how they handle "hippopotamus." "I Wish I Was" was written by Gary Rosen and Bill Shontz. *(All)*

"If I Could Be Anything." Pelham, Ruth. Under One Sky.

Pelham sings that she would be happy to be with you even if she was a raindrop, a pair of argyle socks, or a garden shovel. Add your own verses to this pretty call-and-response song. Pelham's song "If I Could Be Anyone," from the same recording, finds her imagining what it would be like to be Harriet Tubman, Paul Robeson, or Susan B. Anthony. *(All)*

"Late Last Night." Scruggs, Joe. Late Last Night.

Kids can pretend to wear a variety of footwear "late at night."

Late last night while you were asleep,
Someone put some springs on your feet.

Boing! Boing! You sprang out of bed,
And you jumped so high,
You almost hit your head.

Ballet slippers let the kids tippie-toe around the room, and cowboy boots encourage them to gallop. There are also ice skates, flip-flops, moccasins, roller skates, tap shoes, cleats, and cycle boots in this long but creative song. "Late Last Night" was written by Joe and Linda Scruggs.　　*(Ps)*

"Puffy Clouds." Foote, Norman. If the Shoe Fits.

Play Foote's recording while holding up illustrations from Peter Spier's picture book *Dreams*. Both the song and book describe shapes one can visualize in the clouds.　　*(Ps, Pr)*

"Would You Like to Swing on a Star?" Muldaur, Maria. On the Sunny Side.

Children can make mule, pig, and fish noises while listening to the recording. Muldaur's version is a little more laid-back than the other renditions. Hold up pictures or puppets of the above animals as they are mentioned in the song. The song was written by J. Burke and J. Van Heusen. It can also be found under the title "Swinging on a Star" on:
> Bartels, Joanie. Sillytime Magic.
> Feinstein, Michael. Pure Imagination.
> Pease, Tom. Boogie Boogie Boogie.　　*(All)*

Here are more great songs about imagination:

"Big Rock Candy Mountain." Chapin, Tom. Family Tree.

"Big Rock Candy Mountain." Grammer, Red. Red Grammer's Favorite Sing Along Songs.

"Big Rock Candy Mountain." Ives, Burl. The Best of Burl's for Boys and Girls.

"Big Rock Candy Mountain." Wee Sing Fun 'n' Folk.

"Blanketville." Chapin, Tom. Family Tree.

"Can You Show Us." Parachute Express. Sunny Side Up.

"Do You Know What Magic Is?" Arnold, Linda. Make Believe.

"Dreamcatcher." Herdman, Priscilla. Daydreamer.

"Hey Daddy." (Anne Murray) A Child's Celebration of Song.

"House at Pooh Corner." McCornack, Mike and Carleen. Beasties, Bumbershoots, and Lullabies.

"House at Pooh Corner." Rosenshontz. It's the Truth.

"Imaginary Friend." McCutcheon, John. Family Garden.

"Imagination." Penner, Fred. What a Day!

"Imagination." Rosenshontz. Rosenshontz Tickles You.

"Listen to Me." Harley, Bill. Big Big World.

"Make-Believe Day." Rory. Make-Believe Day.

"Make-Believe Town." Peter, Paul and Mary. Peter, Paul and Mommy.

"Monster." Grammer, Red. Can You Sound Just Like Me?

"Monster Day." Arnold, Linda. Peppermint Wings.

"The Monster Song." Tickle Tune Typhoon. Circle Around.

"Monsters Never Comb Their Hair." Atkinson, Lisa. The One and Only Me.

"Monsters on Vacation." Phipps, Bonnie. Monsters' Holiday.

"Mr. Wizard Lizard." Arnold, Linda. Peppermint Wings.

"My Backyard." Block, Cathy. Timeless.

"My Unicorn." McCornack, Mike and Carleen. Beasties, Bumbershoots, and Lullabies.

"No One." Rogers, Sally. What Can One Little Person Do?

"Over the Rainbow." (J. C. Lodge) Reggae for Kids.

"Over the Rainbow." Rory. Make-Believe Day.

"Over the Rainbow." Rosenshontz. It's the Truth.

"Over the Rainbow." Schneider, Bob. When You Dream a Dream.

"Over the Rainbow." Tickle Tune Typhoon. Hearts and Hands.

"The Pocket Song." Rory. Make-Believe Day.

"Pure Imagination." Feinstein, Michael. Pure Imagination.

"Purple People Eater." Bishop, Heather. Purple People Eater.

"Read a Book." Arnold, Linda. Peppermint Wings.

"Something in My Shoe." Raffi. Rise and Shine.

"Somewhere over the Rainbow." Bishop, Heather. Purple People Eater.

"Thumbelina." Raffi. Rise and Shine.

"The Unicorn." Cowboy Steff. The Giving Tree and Other Shel Silverstein Songs.

"The Unicorn Song." Abell, Timmy. The Farmer's Market.

"The Unicorn Song." Roth, Kevin. The Secret Journey.

"When I Fly." Wozniak, Doug. Music for Miles of Smiles.

"When You Dream a Dream." Schneider, Bob. When You Dream a Dream.

"World of Make-Believe." Parachute Express. Feel the Music.

"Zoom." Noah, Tim. In Search of the Wow Wow Wibble Woggle Wazzie Woodle Woo!

Insects

* **"The Ants Go Marching." Wee Sing Silly Songs.**

Make an ant stick puppet by fastening black felt circles on Popsicle sticks. Have the children march these puppets around the room. "The Parade" by Joe Scruggs, from his recording *Ants,* contains new verses to this traditional tune. "The Ants Go Marching" can also be found on:
Sharon, Lois and Bram. Singing 'n Swinging. **(Ps, Pr)**

"Blue Tail Fly." (Rick Danko) American Children.

Rick Danko, of the rock group The Band, sings a nice, easy rendition of this traditional song. The song describes a tragedy that occurs as a result of a fly bite. Greg and Steve's version "Jimmy Crack Corn" on Greg and Steve's *Kidding Around* has little to do with the traditional story, but is a nice variation with lots of movement. The song, titled either "Blue Tail Fly" or "Jimmy Crack Corn," can also be found on:

Abell, Timmy. The Farmer's Market.
Ives, Burl. The Best of Burl's for Boys and Girls.
Seeger, Mike and Peggy. American Folk Songs for
 Children.
Wee Sing and Play.   *(All)*

* **"Boxes of Magic." Peanutbutterjam. Simply Singable.**

The duo Peanutbutterjam (Eileen Packard and Paul Recker)
have boxes of magical fleas, ants, spiders, worms, and bees
that jump, hop, dance, bend, and sit. The children are
encouraged to move accordingly with the creepy crawlies.
"Boxes of Magic" was written by Eileen Packard.   *(Ps, Pr)*

"The Cricket Song." Walker, Mary Lu. The Frog's Party.

Mary Lu Walker's original song is a wonderful match for
Eric Carle's picture book *The Very Quiet Cricket*. The chorus
is easy to sing with the kids chirping away like crickets. Fred
Newman's book *Mouthsounds* teaches you how to make a
realistic cricket noise. (Basically you whistle backwards
through, yuk, a mouthful of spit.)   *(All)*

"Hello Ladybug." Rogers, Sally. Piggyback Planet.

Malvina Reynolds wrote this beautiful song about the
importance of insects and worms in our ecology. The song
is not terribly difficult to learn. Hold up pictures or puppets
of a ladybug, worm, and bee during the appropriate verses.
Dan Crow's "The Best of All Bugs" from his recording *Oops!*
also sings the praises of ladybugs.   *(All)*

* **"Shoo Fly." Ives, Burl. The Best of Burl's
for Boys and Girls.**

Sometimes the simplest activities get the biggest responses
from the little ones. Cut out a felt circle for a fly and attach
it with tape to a piece of string. Dangle the "fly" in front of
a frog puppet while singing the song. I pretend the frog is
singing the song and being pestered by the fly. At the end
of the song, the frog "gulps" the fly. The kids always go into

hysterics. Guaranteed! The traditional "Shoo Fly" can also be found on:

Dallas, Patti, and Laura Baron. Playtime Parade.
Greg and Steve. On the Move.
Sweet Honey in the Rock. I Got Shoes.
Wee Sing Fun 'n' Folk. **(Ps, Pr)**

"The Wooly Booger." Paxton, Tom. Balloon-Alloon-Alloon.

Folkmanis Puppets makes a caterpillar/butterfly puppet that's perfect for this song. Paxton asks if a woolly booger (his name for a caterpillar) is crawling on your toe, knee, chest, and ear. Place the caterpillar puppet on those body parts before it turns into a butterfly. You can use your finger for the caterpillar if you don't have the puppet. Bend your index finger up and down like a caterpillar crawling. When it turns into a butterfly, hold your hands palms out, hook your thumbs, and flap them like butterfly wings. "The Wooly Booger" was written by Paxton. A fun companion song is the traditional "Arabella Miller" by Sharon, Lois and Bram on *Mainly Mother Goose*. Arabella had a caterpillar that crawled on her brother and grandmother. **(Ps)**

Here are more great songs about insects:

"Baby Bumblebee." Wee Sing Silly Songs.

"The Bee and the Pup." Wee Sing Fun 'n' Folk.

"Boll Weevil." Ives, Burl. The Best of Burl's for Boys and Girls.

"Bug Bites." Miché, Mary. Earthy Tunes.

"Bugs." Rosenshontz. Uh-Oh.

"Butterfly, Fly." Buckner, Janice. Everybody's Special.

"The Farm." Scruggs, Joe. Ants.

"A Flea and a Fly in a Flue." Fink, Cathy. Grandma Slid down the Mountain.

"Flea, Fly, Mosquito." Sharon, Lois and Bram. One Elephant, Deux Elephants.

"The Grasshopper's Fiddle." Buckner, Janice. Everybody's Special.

"Grasshoppers Three." Quackity Yakity Bop.

"Never Swat a Fly." Muldaur, Maria. On the Sunny Side.

"No Bones Within." Banana Slug String Band. Adventures on the Air Cycle.

"The Terrible Bug." Pirtle, Sarah. The Wind Is Telling Secrets.

"There Ain't No Bugs on Me." Garcia, Jerry, and Grissman, David. Not for Kids Only.

"The Ugly Bug Ball." Feinstein, Michael. Pure Imagination.

"The Ugly Bugly." Wozniak, Doug. Music for Miles of Smiles.

Movement

"Ants in My Pants." Scruggs, Joe. Late Last Night.

> Scruggs describes the day when ants crawled up his pants and he did a very crazy dance which he named the "I've Got Ants in My Pants Dance." Because of other odd circumstances he also inadvertently does the "I Can't Move Boogaloo," the "Up to Our Chin, Save Yourself Swim," the "Twist and Turn, Wiggle Worm Squirm," the "Crocodile Rock," and more, including my favorite, the "OOOOOH, There's a Snake Shimmy and Shake." Have the children use their imagination and move to Scruggs's directions. "Ants in My Pants" was written by Scruggs. **(Pr)**

* "Clap Your Hands." Tickle Tune Typhoon. Circle Around.

> Clap your hands, wiggle your fingers, flap your arms, shake your shoulders, and slide your feet like James Brown in this melodic movement song. The song is simple enough to sing yourself—or play the recording, which has a fun calypso beat. **(Ps)**

"The Hokey Pokey." Sharon, Lois and Bram. Stay Tuned.

> "The Hokey Pokey" is the most requested song we get at our library. I was never a fan of this song until I witnessed several hundred youngsters spontaneously "hokey pokey" in a

university arena while awaiting the results of a tense Odyssey of the Mind competition. What fun! "The Hokey Pokey" was written by Charles P. Macak, Larry Laprise, and Tafft Baker and can also be found on:

The Chenille Sisters. 1-2-3 for Kids.
Dallas, Patti, and Laura Baron. Good Morning Sunshine.
Greg and Steve. Kidding Around.
Little Richard. Shake It All About.
Tickle Tune Typhoon. All of Us Will Shine.
Wee Sing and Play. **(All)**

"The If You Like Song." Lewis, Shari. Lamb Chop's Sing-Along, Play-Along.

Lewis tells you to wiggle if you like puppies and pinch your nose if you like parties. Lewis also leads the children into barking, oinking, meowing, and blowing kisses in this fun follow-the-directions song. "The If You Like Song" was written by Norman Martin. **(Ps, Pr)**

* "Join in the Game." Greg and Steve. Playing Favorites.

Everyone will be up and clapping, giggling, snoring, hiccuping, and sneezing to this simple Greg and Steve original. The two musicians also lead the children in performing several combinations of activities such as snoring, giggling, and clapping all at once. Add your own verses. **(All)**

"The Journey Dance." Pirtle, Sarah. Magical Earth.

Pirtle acts as a caller leading the children to dance as if they were moving through peanut butter, applesauce, and marshmallows. She also directs the children to turn in a circle, slide, and make a pretzel shape before bowing to their partners and resting their "weary bones." The children will be able to sing the chorus as they dance. "The Journey Dance" was written by Pirtle. **(Pr, I)**

"Jump." Avni, Fran. Artichokes and Brussel Sprouts.

Avni presents a slightly unusual follow-the-directions song. Kids are instructed to jump, stamp, or walk tippy-toe while placing their hands in several positions. Children may find themselves jumping with their hands on their heads and hips or stamping with their hands on their chins and elbows. All in all, songwriter Jackie Cytrynbaum has created a dance version of the popular game Twister. **(All)**

"Jump Children." Marxer, Marcy. Jump Children.

Here is a good song to end your session or class. Marxer asks the children if they want to jump. The children respond with a loud "Yeah" and proceed to jump. She then asks if they want to dance. They again shout "Yeah" and dance. Add your own verses. (See how they respond if you ask them if they want to clean the room.) "Jump Children" was written by Marxer and T. Leonino. It can also be found on:
  Fink, Cathy, and Marcy Marxer. A Cathy and Marcy
  Collection for Kids. **(All)**

* "Shake My Sillies Out." Raffi. More Singable Songs.

"Shake My Sillies Out" is a modern-day classic written by Raffi and Bert and Bonnie Simpson. Many children who visit our library are very familiar with this zipper song. Shake your sillies, clap your crazies, jump your jiggles, yawn your sleepies, or add your own verses. Use Raffi's picture book for smaller and younger groups. "Shake My Sillies Out" can also be found on:
  Cassidy, Nancy. Kids' Songs. **(Ps, Pr)**

"Skip to My Lou." Greg and Steve. We All Live Together, Vol. 1.

Greg and Steve are masters at turning traditional folk songs into fun movement activities. Here they add commands such as "touch your toes, skip to my lou," "flap your wings, skip to my lou," "bang your drum, skip to my lou," and more. Traditional versions of "Skip to My Lou" can be found on:
  Cappelli, Frank. Pass the Coconut.
  Carfra, Pat. Babes, Beasts, and Birds.
  A Child's Celebration of Song. (John McCutcheon)

Family Folk Festival. (John McCutcheon)
Fink, Cathy. When the Rain Comes Down.
Penner, Fred. A House for Me.
Seeger, Mike and Peggy. American Folk Songs for
   Children.
Sharon, Lois and Bram. Mainly Mother Goose.
Wee Sing and Play.   *(All)*

**"This Little Light of Mine." Drake, David HB.
Kid-Stuff.**

Drake adds movement activities to this traditional song.
"These little hands of mine, I'm gonna make them clap."
This pattern song also includes having these little feet
dance, eyes blink, noses twitch, and heads shake. What
other ideas can you and the children add?   *(Ps, Pr)*

**"The Turning Song." Lewis, Shari. Lamb Chop's
Sing-Along, Play-Along.**

Not only will the children turn faster and faster as the
music plays, but they will also jump, hop, wiggle, and clap.
This song has more aerobics than a Jane Fonda workout
tape. "The Turning Song" was written by Norman Martin.
                                               (Ps, Pr)

* "Walkin'." Sharon, Lois and Bram. Stay Tuned.

Kids can add their own movement verses to this traditional
pattern song. "Walkin', I'm just walkin' along. I'm just singin' my walkin' song. I'm just walkin' along." Replace the
word walkin' with jumpin', hoppin', skippin', or any other
"-in'" movement. Perform it as a circle song.   *(Ps, Pr)*

*** "A Walking We Will Go." Greg and Steve.
We All Live Together, Vol. 5.**

Greg and Steve lead kids into walking, stomping, skipping,
sliding, bouncing, tip-toeing, and marching to the tune of
"A Hunting We Will Go." The song was adapted by Greg
Scelsa.   *(Ps, Pr)*

"The Wiggle Song." Whiteley, Ken. All of the Seasons.

A mermaid wiggles, the kids will wiggle, even the organ playing on the recording wiggles. My own kids couldn't help but wiggle when they heard this lively recording. "The Wiggle Song" was written by Whiteley and his son Ben.

(Ps, Pr)

Here are more great movement songs:

"Body Groove." Kinnoin, David. Daring Dewey.

"Body Machine." Buckner, Janice. Little Friends for Little Folks.

"Clothesline Hop." Atkinson, Lisa. The One and Only Me.

"Copy Cat." Greg and Steve. Kidding Around.

"Dance." Block, Cathy. Timeless.

"Dance Around." Guthrie, Woody. Woody's 20 Grow Big Songs.

"Dance, Puppet, Dance." Parachute Express. Feel the Music.

"Doin' the Robot." Tickle Tune Typhoon. Hug the Earth.

"The Freeze." Greg and Steve. Kids in Motion.

"Get Up, Get Down, Go Crazy." Bennett, Glenn. I Must Be Growing.

"Get Up, Get Down, Go Crazy." (Glenn Bennett) Early Ears: Songs Just for 4 Year Olds.

"Giggle Tickle Fiddle Little Wiggle Around." Polisar, Barry Louis. Old Dog, New Tricks.

"Got the Rhythm." Tickle Tune Typhoon. Hug the Earth.

"Heartbeat Drumbeat." Bartels, Joanie. Jump for Joy.

"Hey, Betty Martin." Buchman, Rachel. Hello Everybody.

"Hey, Good Buddy." Gibson, Dee, and Joe Scruggs. Songs to Brighten Your Day.

"In the Dancing." Berman, Marcia. Marcia Berman Sings Malvina Reynolds' Rabbits Dance.

"Jim Along Josie." Parachute Express. Shakin' It!

"Jim Along Josie." Penner, Fred. Fred Penner's Place.

"Jim Along Josie." Seeger, Mike and Peggy. American Folk Songs for Children.

"Jump for Joy." Bartels, Joanie. Jump for Joy.

"Kids in Motion." Greg and Steve. Kids in Motion.

"Knees Up Mother Brown." Cassidy, Nancy. Kids' Songs Jubilee.

"Knees Up Mother Brown." Raffi. Raffi in Concert with the Rise and Shine Band.

"My Young Friend." Cappelli, Frank. Pass the Coconut.

"Old Brass Wagon." Greg and Steve. We All Live Together, Vol. 5.

"Ready Set." Grammer, Red. Can You Sound Just like Me?

"Round in a Circle." Greg and Steve. We All Live Together, Vol. 1.

"Shake It Up." Monet, Lisa. My Best Friend.

"Smooth Movin' Boogie Express." Parachute Express. Happy to Be Here.

"Try to Fly." Avni, Fran. Artichokes and Brussel Sprouts.

"Use Your Own Two Feet." Marxer, Marcy. Jump Children.

"Wiggle Wobble." Greg and Steve. We All Live Together, Vol. 1.

Music

* "I'm in the Mood." Raffi. Rise and Shine.

> Raffi wrote this very simple song that is ready-made for children to add their own verses. Raffi sings that he is in the mood for singing, clapping, whistling, and stomping. What other musical activities can you add (humming, dancing)?
> *(Ps, Pr)*

"The Kitchen Percussion Song." The Chenille Sisters. 1-2-3 for Kids.

> Break out the kitchen utensils and let the children play them as rhythm instruments. There are places in the song for them to bang their spoons, pots, and pans. "The Kitchen Percussion Song" was written by group members Connie Huber and Grace Morand. *(Ps, Pr)*

"Momma Don't Allow." Arnold, Linda. Happiness Cake.

Read Thacher Hurd's picture book *Mama Don't Allow* starring Milo and the Swamp Band. Play Arnold's rollicking recording afterward. The children will soon be laughing, clapping, singing, and playing the spoons, pots, pans, and kazoos. This traditional song can also be found on:
    Nagler, Eric. Fiddle Up a Tune. *(All)*

"Old King Cole." Wellington, Bill. WOOF Hits the Road.

Wellington has found an interesting, but not well-known, version of the nursery rhyme. Old King Cole not only calls for his fiddlers, he also calls for his fifers, drummers, harpoons, weavers, farmers, and preachers. The result is a fast-paced, cumulative, tongue-twister full of sound effects. You can teach the children to learn one sound effect and have them stand up for their turn. Some will say " 'gee-whoa-haw,' said the farmers," others will say " 'ring-dang-doodle,' said the harpoons," and so on. Slow it down from Wellington's rapid-fire pace until you've mastered the timing. A great challenge for a music class. The same version can also be found on:
    Wellington, Bill. WOOF's Greatest Bits. *(Pr, I)*

**"Old MacDonald Had a Band." Raffi. Singable Songs
for the Very Young.**

Raffi's version includes a banjo, guitar, jug, fiddle, and singers instead of farm animals. Even though Raffi uses real instruments on the recording, kids can imitate these sounds with their mouths. They can also add their own instruments to this cumulative song. *(Ps, Pr)*

**"Playtime Parade." Dallas, Patti, and Laura Baron.
Playtime Parade.**

This marching song written by Laura Baron introduces children to the flute, tuba, trombone, and drums. Teach them to pantomime the playing of each instrument and let them march around the room while listening to the recording. Red Grammer's song "Big Brass Band" from his recording

Can You Sound Just like Me? accomplishes virtually the same effect with the addition of cymbals. **(Ps, Pr)**

* **"Ricky Ticky Song." Cowboy Steff. The Giving Tree and Other Shel Silverstein Songs.**

Shel Silverstein's pattern song uses nonsense lyrics to entice children to sing. Cowboy Steff teaches them how to sing a "ricky ticky" song, a "scooby-dooby" song, and a "yugga-lugga" song. Add your own verses with the children, such as a "wiggly-giggly" song or a "humpety-dumpety" song. **(All)**

"Shaker Song." Pelham, Ruth. Under One Sky.

Pelham's simple musical directions describe how to put gravel into an egg carton to create a rhythm instrument. Bring supplies for the kids and have them play their shakers to the music. Pelham does virtually the same thing with her song "Guitar Box Band" from the same recording. A good companion song on which the children can play their shakers is Eric Nagler's "You Just Improvise" from his recording *Improvise with Eric Nagler.* Nagler admonishes his orchestra for getting out of hand during this hilarious song. In addition to playing their shakers, the kids will have a chance to play a wax paper/comb solo. **(Ps, Pr)**

* **"This Little Song." Lewis, Shari. Lamb Chop's Sing-Along, Play-Along.**

As Lamb Chop says, there are many ways to sing this song. If a chicken sang it, it would sound like "bok-bok-bok." Lewis also uses bells and cats for this pattern song. Ask the children to add their own verses. The possibilities are endless. "This Little Song" was written by Norman Martin. **(All)**

* **"You Gotta Sing." Raffi. More Singable Songs.**

You gotta sing, dance, shout, wiggle, and shake when the spirit moves you. Add your own verses to this traditional pattern song. "You Gotta Sing" can also be found on:

Cassidy, Nancy. Kids' Songs.
Gemini. Pulling Together.
Tickle Tune Typhoon. Hearts and Hands (listed in this album as "Sing When the Spirit Says Sing"). *(All)*

* **"You'll Sing a Song and I'll Sing a Song." Jenkins, Ella. You'll Sing a Song and I'll Sing a Song.**

Jenkins wrote this simple, melodic, and infectious tune. She sings that we'll sing, play, and whistle a tune together. Ask the children to make up new verses such as "You'll clap your hands and I'll clap my hands and we'll clap our hands together." "You'll Sing a Song and I'll Sing a Song" can also be found on:
Raffi. Corner Grocery Store. *(Ps, Pr)*

Here are more great songs about music:

"All Star Band." Wozniak, Doug. Hugs and Kisses.
"Band of Sounds." Schneider, Bob. When You Dream a Dream.
"Busy Box Band." Scruggs, Joe. Bahamas Pajamas.
"Down the Do-Re-Mi." Grammer, Red. Down the Do-Re-Mi.
"Feel the Music." Parachute Express. Feel the Music.
"Gonna Have a Good Time." Rosenshontz. Share It.
"Grandma Slid down the Mountain." Fink, Cathy. Grandma Slid down the Mountain.
"Ha Ha This-a-Way." Sharon, Lois and Bram. Mainly Mother Goose.
"The Harmony Song." The Chenille Sisters. 1-2-3 for Kids.
"Hey Dum Diddeley Dum." Sharon, Lois and Bram. Great Big Hits.
"Hey Dum Diddeley Dum." Sharon, Lois and Bram. Smorgasbord.
"Hey Dum Diddle Dum." Foote, Norman. Foote Prints.
"Hey Dum Diddley Dum." Cassidy, Nancy. Kids' Songs 2.
"Hey Ev'rybody." Alsop, Peter. Take Me with You.

"I Have a Song to Sing, O!" Peter, Paul and Mary. Peter, Paul and Mommy.

"Is There Anybody Here?" Sharon, Lois and Bram. One Elephant, Deux Elephants.

"It's Music to Me." The Flyers. Your Smile.

"Jambonee." (Happy Traum) American Children.

"Jubilee." Cassidy, Nancy. Kids' Songs Jubilee.

"La-La Man." Parachute Express. Circle of Friends.

"Let's Make Some Noise." Raffi. Everything Grows.

"The Little Shekere." Sweet Honey in the Rock. All for Freedom.

"Making Music." Tickle Tune Typhoon. Hearts and Hands.

"The Mandolin Song." Rosenshontz. Share It.

"One Sweet Song." Rosenshontz. Rosenshontz Tickles You.

"Rock around the World." Pease, Tom. I'm Gonna Reach.

"Rounds." Chapin, Tom. Family Tree.

"Scat like That." Greg and Steve. On the Move.

"Sing a Happy Song." Rosenshontz. Rosenshontz Tickles You.

"Sing Sing Sing." Penner, Fred. Fred Penner's Place.

"Singin'." (Glenn Bennett) Early Ears: Songs Just for 2 Year Olds.

"Time to Sing." Raffi. One Light, One Sun.

"Time to Sing." Raffi. Raffi in Concert with the Rise and Shine Band.

"Try It, You'll Like It." Bartels, Joanie. Jump for Joy.

Names

"Eddie Coochie." Phipps, Bonnie. Dinosaur Choir.

"Eddie Coochie" is very similar to Arlene Mosel's picture book *Tikki Tikki Tembo*. Both song and book feature boys who fall into wells and have trouble getting out because of their long names. Eddie's full name is "Eddie Coochie

Cacha Cama Tosa Nara Tosa Noka Sama Whacky Brown."
(That's as close as I can get it.) The children will be up for
the challenge of learning this long name as well as Tikki
Tikki Tembo's. Write it out for them to see. Read the book,
then play the recording. **(All)**

"Everybody Eats When They Come to My House." Sharon, Lois and Bram. Happy Birthday.

Rhyme children's names with food items in this bouncy
song written by Jeanne Burns. Sharon, Lois and Bram
match salami with Tommy, gravy with Davey, chili con
carne with Arnie, banana with Hannah, spumoni with
Tony, and even taffy with Raffi. See what rhyming combinations your children can make. **(Pr, I)**

* "Hey Lolly, Lolly." Wee Sing Sing-Alongs.

You can spend a lot of time with the children in your care
with this traditional name song. "I know a boy [or girl]
named [say one of the children's names]. He [state something that rhymes with the child's name]." For example,
sing "I know a boy named Mike. Hey, lolly lolly-o. He likes
to ride a bike. Hey lolly lolly-o." Be forewarned that many
names are very challenging to rhyme. Be prepared to go a
long ways to stretch the rhymes. "I know a girl named
Jessica. Hey lolly, lolly-o. She wore a pretty vest-ica. Hey
lolly, lolly-o." (Also be prepared for a lot of groans from any
adults in the audience.) **(Ps, Pr)**

* "I See a Horsie." Weissman, Jackie. Peanut Butter, Tarzan, and Roosters.

Start with animal names and noises for this pattern song. "I
see a cow, what does it say? Moo!" Weissman moves on to
children's names with wonderful results. "I see a [fill in
someone's name]." Then ask them to say something.
They'll say "hi" or "um" or something surprising. For example, you might sing "I see a Aaron, what does he say? He
says 'Hee-hee.'" This is probably how Art Linkletter got his
start for his "Kids Say the Darndest Things." **(Ps)**

"Madalina Catalina." Phipps, Bonnie. Monsters' Holiday.

Like the song "Eddie Coochie" (listed above), Phipps has recorded a tongue-twisting name song that will be a challenge for the children to learn. Madalina's full name is Madalina Catalina Hoopensteiner Wallendiner Hogan Bogan Logan. Phipps sings the name at various speeds which adds to the fun. This traditional song can be found as "Magelena Hagelena" on:
> Wellington, Bill. WOOF Hits Home.
> Wellington, Bill. WOOF's Greatest Bits.   ***(Pr, I)***

* "Share." Palmer, Hap. Babysong.

This sharing song is a good way to learn the names of the young children in your group. Place each child's name in this pattern song. Simply say the name of one child, ask them what their favorite toy or possession is, and ask them to share it with the child next to them. "Andrew, share your trucks with Michael." "Mei-Ling, share your bat and ball with Matthew." "Share" was written by Palmer and Martha Cheney.   ***(Ps)***

* "Willoughby Wallaby Woo." Raffi. Singable Songs for the Very Young.

Raffi adapted this song based on a Dennis Lee poem from the book *Alligator Pie* and set to music by Larry Miyata. Take a child's name and substitute a "w" for the first consonant of their name. If the child's name begins with a vowel, add the "w" to the beginning of the name. Thus, Alice becomes "Walice," Jayne becomes "Wayne," Julia becomes "Wulia," Laura becomes "Waura," and Sam becomes "Wam." Not all children are comfortable with changing their names into nonsensical rhymes, so be sure to ask them first. I always use my own name first as an example (that's "Wob" in Willoughby Wallaby lingo). I usually end the song by changing the name of the library or school we are at, such as the "Winneapolis Wublic Wibrary." "Willoughby Wallaby Woo" can also be found on:
> Cassidy, Nancy. Kids' Songs.   ***(All)***

Here are more great songs about names:

"I Hate My Name." Charette, Rick. Where Do My Sneakers Go at Night?

"John Jacob Jingleheimer Schmidt." Sharon, Lois and Bram. All the Fun You Can Sing!

"John Jacob Jingleheimer Schmidt." Sharon, Lois and Bram. Smorgasbord.

"Jump into the Circle." Monet, Lisa. Circle Time.

"Like Me and You." Raffi. One Light, One Sun.

"Like Me and You." Raffi. Raffi in Concert with the Rise and Shine Band.

"The Name Game." Bartels, Joanie. Sillytime Magic.

"The Name Game." Bishop, Heather. Purple People Eater.

"The Name Game." The Chenille Sisters. The Big Picture.

"Zachary Zack." Foote, Norman. If the Shoe Fits.

Nonsense

"Come and Make a Rhyme." Peanutbutterjam. Peanutbutterjam Goes to School.

> This Eileen Packard composition conjures up several images similar to the "Down by the Bay" song listed below. A deer with bologna in its ear and a rat cooking spaghetti in a hat are just two of the nonsense rhymes made.　　**(Ps, Pr)**

"Down by the Bay." Raffi. Singable Songs for the Very Young.

> My friends Linda Fink and Cynthia Hanson of the Hudson (Wis.) Public Library hold up pictures they made of the silly images found in this traditional song. These include pictures of a whale with a polka dot tail, a fly wearing a tie, a goose kissing a moose, a bear combing its hair, and llamas eating their pajamas. The drawings were laminated for long-term wear and tear. If you don't know of an adult with

the least bit of artistic talent, ask the children to draw the pictures. They'll do an amazing job. Or hold up Raffi's picture book of the same name. "Down by the Bay" can also be found on:

> Cassidy, Nancy. Kids' Songs.
> Greg and Steve. Playing Favorites.
> Roth, Kevin. Dinosaurs, Dragons, and Other Children's Songs.
> Roth, Kevin. Travel Song Sing Alongs.
> Wee Sing Silly Songs. *(Ps, Pr)*

"I Know an Old Lady Who Swallowed a Fly." Peter, Paul and Mary. Peter, Paul and Mommy, Too.

Peter, Paul and Mary's concert version is very comical, complete with an Elvis impersonation. The audience tries to challenge them by suggesting new things for the lady to swallow and see if the trio can make a rhyme. My personal contributions are "I know an old lady who swallowed a dinosaur. Oh, she was very, very sore" and "I know an old lady who swallowed a whale. That's the end of this tale." Be sure to check out Bernice Nadine Westcott's picture book version of the same title. Other versions of this traditional song can be found on:

> Ives, Burl. The Best of Burl's for Boys and Girls.
> Penner, Fred, Ebeneezer Sneezer.
> Roth, Kevin. Travel Song Sing Alongs.
> Roth, Kevin. Unbearable Bears.
> Seeger, Peter. Stories and Songs for Children. *(All)*

* "I Think I'll Try Some." Buchman, Rachel. Hello Everybody.

Buchman's original simple song draws lots of laughter whenever we use it in storytime. She sings that little girls and little boys shouldn't eat things like houses, sidewalks, cars, refrigerators, spaceships, lawn mowers, alligators, guitars, and mommies. But she also sings that she'll try some. Have the children add their own silly suggestions. *(Ps, Pr)*

"Plenty of Room." Chapin, Tom. Family Tree.

Remember the '50s craze of cramming college students into a phone booth? Chapin does it even better by squeezing several friends, a choir, fire trucks, and St. Bernards into a phone booth. Play the recording of this cumulative song for the wonderful sound effects. The children can join the last two lines of the chorus. "Plenty of Room" was written by Chapin and John Forster. *(Pr, I)*

"The Woman Who Gobbled Swiss Cheese." Pirtle, Sarah. Two Hands Hold the Earth.

Judy Sierra's *The Flannel Board Storytelling Book* has several patterns for a felt woman. Choose one and use it for this hilarious song. A woman swallows Swiss cheese and as a result develops holes in her knees. Her remedy to swallow green tiddlywinks backfires when green circles appear on her knees. Make the felt woman with removable circles at her knees, a felt chunk of Swiss cheese (a yellow rectangle or triangle with circles drawn on it), and green circles for the tiddlywinks. Manipulate the felt figures as you play the recording. "The Woman Who Gobbled Swiss Cheese" was written by Pirtle and can also be found on:
Winter, Cathy, and Betsy Rose. As Strong as Anyone Can Be. *(All)*

* "Yes, I Can!" Peanutbutterjam. Simply Singable.

Paul Recker of Peanutbutterjam sings nonsensical statements like you can't fry eggs in bathroom sinks or you can't put teachers in mayonnaise jars. The children shout "Yes, I can!" after each line. Make up your own silly statements. And then make sure you have scheduled a lot of time for this Eileen Packard song. *(All)*

Here are more great nonsense songs:

"Acorn Brown." Sharon, Lois and Bram. Stay Tuned.
"The Ballad of Lucy Lumm." Phipps, Bonnie. Monsters' Holiday.

"Chicken Lips and Lizard Hips." Cassidy, Nancy. Kids' Songs.

"Cindy." Nagler, Eric. Fiddle Up a Tune.

"Cornstalk Fiddle." Nagler, Eric. Fiddle Up a Tune.

"Daddy's Whiskers." Nagler, Eric. Improvise with Eric Nagler.

"The Donut Song." Ives, Burl. Little White Duck.

"Father's Old Grey Whiskers." Cassidy, Nancy. Kids' Songs.

"Father's Whiskers." Wee Sing Silly Songs.

"Hopalong Peter." Garcia, Jerry, and David Grissman. Not for Kids Only.

"Hopalong Peter." Nagler, Eric. Come On In.

"A Horse Named Bill." Garcia, Jerry, and David Grissman. Not for Kids Only.

"I Am Slowly Going Crazy." Sharon, Lois and Bram. Singing 'n Swinging.

"Jig Along Home." Guthrie, Woody. Woody's 20 Grow Big Songs.

"Jig Along Home." Raffi. Corner Grocery Store.

"Little Liza Jane." Sharon, Lois and Bram. Stay Tuned.

"Oh Me Oh My." Raffi. More Singable Songs.

"On Top of Spaghetti." Little Richard. Shake It All About.

"Risseldy Rosseldy." Wee Sing Silly Songs.

"Silly Song." Bishop, Heather. Purple People Eater.

"Silly Song." Livingston, Bob. Open the Window.

"Sing in the Spring." Diamond, Charlotte. Diamond in the Rough.

"Sing Song Kitty." Watson, Doc. Doc Watson Sings Songs for Little Pickers.

"Something in My Shoe." Raffi. Rise and Shine.

"There Was a Man and He Was Mad." Seeger, Mike and Peggy. American Folk Songs for Children.

"The Three Jolly Huntsmen." Ives, Burl. The Best of Burl's for Boys and Girls.

"Three Men Went A-Hunting." Garcia, Jerry, and David Grissman. Not for Kids Only.

"Tick Tock." Arnold, Linda. Make Believe.

"Willy Falldown." Parachute Express. Happy to Be Here.

"Zag Zig." Chapin, Tom. Zag Zig.

Plants

"Branching Out." Pease, Tom. I'm Gonna Reach.

John Gorka wrote this inspirational song about wishing to be a tree. There's a lot of humor concerning dogs getting too close and fears of turning into a Louisville Slugger. Have the children reach as high as they can as if their arms, hands, and fingers were the branches of a tree. They can chime in on the "I'm gonna reach" echo. "Branching Out" can also be found on:

Herdman, Priscilla. Daydreamer.   ***(Pr, I)***

"Five Green Apples." Sharon, Lois and Bram.
Mainly Mother Goose.

Make five green felt apples and one felt tree. Take the apples off one by one as Farmer Brown plucks them from the tree. A similar song is "Five Little Leaves" from Fran Avni's *Daisies and Ducklings*. Make five colorful felt leaves and remove them from the tree one by one as the wind blows them down. The children can make blowing noises. There are several apple, tree, and leaf patterns in *Felt Board Fun* by Liz and Dick Wilmes.   ***(Ps)***

"The Giving Tree." Cowboy Steff. The Giving Tree
and Other Shel Silverstein Songs.

Shel Silverstein's book *The Giving Tree* is a great match for this song, which he also wrote. Read the book first, then play this melodic song. Another song that goes well with the book is Troubadour's "Tree Song" from *On the Trail*. Troubadour's song is about playing with "my friend tree."   ***(All)***

"Hole in the Middle of the Tree." Avni, Fran. Daisies
   and Ducklings.

   Avni has created a variation of the traditional song "There's
   a Hole in the Bottom of the Sea." Bark beetle, bumblebee,
   mouse, woodpecker, squirrel, and raccoon are all gathered
   around a hole in the middle of a tree. The cumulative song
   lends itself to a draw-and-tell presentation for those with
   artistic talent.   *(Ps, Pr)*

* "I'm a Tree." Banana Slug String Band. Dirt Made
   My Lunch.

   A deep "tree" voice sings this simple, cumulative song that
   is full of sounds children can make. Wind, bird, and squirrel noises can be made while they listen to the advantages
   of having a tree around. The kids will be giggling throughout the song, especially if you stand straight and tall holding branches in each hand. "I'm a Tree" was written by
   Steve Van Zandt.   *(Ps, Pr)*

"Lotta Seeds Grow." Miché, Mary. Earthy Tunes.

   A lot of things like trees start out small and grow very tall.
   Write the lyrics of this pattern song for the children to read.
   Underline the word "trees." Substitute this word with other
   things that grow with care. Miché sings about flowers, corn,
   stories, songs, kids, and love as things that can grow from
   "seeds so small." Written by T. Hunter.   *(All)*

"My Roots Go Down." Pirtle, Sarah. Two Hands
   Hold the Earth.

   Pirtle sings about being a pine tree, a willow, a wildflower,
   and a waterfall. Each verse is repeated three times to invite
   the whole group to sing along. The children can add their
   own images to this simple, pattern song. "My Roots Go
   Down" was written by Pirtle and can also be found on:
      O'Brien, Bruce. In My Family's House.
      Pease, Tom. Wobbi-Do-Wop.   *(All)*

* **"Pussy Willow Riddle."** Buchman, Rachel. Hello Everybody.

> This traditional song is all about the pussy that will never be a cat. Buchman tells the children that they can sing this song with their whole bodies. She directs them to crouch and slowly grow (stand up) as the song progresses. The song is short, but the very young love it. **(Ps)**

"That's What the Daisy Said." Sharon, Lois and Bram. Stay Tuned.

> Make a large, ten-petal felt daisy. The song follows the pattern of the saying "She [or he] loves me, she loves me not." Play the recording and remove the petals as the singer counts each one. Put the petals back the second time the song is sung. Explain to the children the superstition of plucking the petals off a flower to predict one's love. **(All)**

Here are more great songs about plants:

"Apple Picker's Reel." Herdman, Priscilla. Daydreamer.

"Apple Picker's Reel." Sharon, Lois and Bram. One, Two, Three, Four, Live!

"Big Red Rap." Banana Slug String Band. Adventures on the Air Cycle.

"Dandelion." Rosen, Gary. Tot Rock.

"Dandelions." Atkinson, Lisa. I Wanna Tickle the Fish.

"Each of Us Is a Flower." Diamond, Charlotte. 10 Carrot Diamond.

"Family Trees." Scooter. Calling All Kids.

"From a Seed in the Ground." Bishop, Heather. Bellybutton.

"Giant Kelp Forest." Banana Slug String Band. Slugs at Sea.

"A Little Acorn." The Chenille Sisters. The Big Picture.

"Little Tree." Lonnquist, Ken. Welcome 2 Kenland.

"Plant More Than You Harvest." (Rory) Put on Your Green Shoes.

"Roots, Stems, Leaves." Banana Slug String Band. Dirt Made My Lunch.

"Six Plant Parts." Miché, Mary. Earthy Tunes.

"Sprites." Pirtle, Sarah. The Wind Is Telling Secrets.

"Thank a Plant." Janet and Judy. Musical Almanac.

"Tree Counting Song." Bethie. Bethie's Really Silly Songs about Numbers.

"Tree Dancin'." Tickle Tune Typhoon. Circle Around.

"Tree Song." Troubadour. On the Trail.

"Treemendous." Wozniak, Doug. Hugs and Kisses.

"Trees." Avni, Fran. Daisies and Ducklings.

"Trees." The Van Manens. Healthy Planet, Healthy People.

"Tulips and Daisies." Avni, Fran. Daisies and Ducklings.

"Up in a Tree." Lonnquist, Ken. Welcome 2 Kenland.

"What Kind of Tree Are You?" Diamond, Charlotte. Diamond in the Rough.

"White Coral Bells." Herdman, Priscilla. Daydreamer.

"Wild Mountain Thyme." Cassidy, Nancy. Kids' Songs Jubilee.

"Wild, Wild Party in the Loquat Tree." (Indigo Girls) Put on Your Green Shoes.

"Wildflowers." Diamond, Charlotte. My Bear Gruff.

School

"Don't Make Me." Chapin, Tom. Family Tree.

Chapin and John Forster wrote a dirge about the tragedy of going to school. The singer starts off complaining about being sick, but quickly changes tactics and promises mom he will do the dishes and wash the dog if she'll let him stay home. This hilarious song is set to the music of Tchaikovsky. Good for a music class studying this classical composer. *(I)*

"Excuses." Troubadour. On the Trail.

Judith Steinbergh and Victor Cockburn, who make up Troubadour, wrote this song about a kid's panic attack upon realizing his homework is missing. The chorus is very catchy. Play the recording and then read Jack Prelutsky's poem "Homework! Oh, Homework" from his book *The New Kid on the Block*. Another poem to read with this song is Kalli Dakos's "A Teacher's Lament" from Bruce Lansky's book *Kids Pick the Funniest Poems*. The teacher in this poem does not want to hear the students' excuses, especially since she left her own work at home.   *(I)*

"I Don't Wanna Go to School." Polisar, Barry Louis. Teacher's Favorites.

This is the funniest school song I've ever heard. Tommy doesn't want to go to school; his mother insists. The surprise ending gets laughs every time. (Hint: Invite your school's principal to listen to this Polisar original.) Another school song with a surprise ending is Joe Scruggs's "First Day" from *Even Trolls Have Moms*. "I Don't Wanna Go to School" can also be found on:
Polisar, Barry Louis. Family Concert.   *(Pr, I)*

"Kindergarten Wall." McCutcheon, John. Mail Myself to You.

McCutcheon's song was inspired by the book *All I Really Need to Know I Learned in Kindergarten* by Robert Fulghum. Little lessons we learned in kindergarten should always remain with us.

> *Of all you learned here, remember this the best,*
> *don't hurt each other and clean up your mess.*
> *Take a nap every day, wash before you eat,*
> *hold hands, stick together, look before you cross the*
> *   street.*
> *And remember the seed in the little paper cup,*
> *First the root goes down and then the plant grows up.*

Post these wise words on your own wall. "Kindergarten Wall" can also be found on:

Abell, Timmy. *Play All Day.*

Herdman, Priscilla. *Daydreamer.*   *(Pr)*

"Nothing." Polisar, Barry Louis. Teacher's Favorites.

What do the kids usually say when their parents ask them what they learned at school that day? "Nothing!" This funny Polisar composition has several opportunities for your kids to shout "Nothing!" The group Troubadour also recorded a song in which kids can shout "Nothing!" over and over. Their song "What Did You Do at School Today?" can be found on their recording *Are We Almost There?*

(Pr, I)

"These Are the Questions." Rosenshontz. Rosenshontz Tickles You.

Rosenshontz asks questions that kids are apt to ask. Is the sun ever cold? Do teeth talk? Do oceans make sand? All the questions they ask have "No!" for the answer. The kids will soon catch on and have their "No!" ready to shout. *(Pr, I)*

"Too Sick for School." Nagler, Eric. Come On In.

Nagler sings about being too sick to go to the school where teachers give horrible spelling tests, teach complicated grammar rules, and send you to the dungeon if you're wrong. The kids can join the catchy chorus when Nagler sings that he really needs to stay in bed all day. (At least until school is out and the pain begins to leave.) Share this song with Shel Silverstein's poem "Sick" from the book *Where the Sidewalk Ends.*   *(Pr, I)*

"A Wee Bit Weird." Neat, Roxanne, and David Stoeri. The Bell Cow Swing.

Stoeri (who used to teach sixth grade) pokes gentle fun at sixth-graders by singing that they eat june-bug pancakes and are getting so old they wear false teeth. Meanwhile, he brags how good the other grades are because they eat healthy food and are in tip-top condition. At the end of the song, Stoeri admits that the sixth-graders are really "blue-ribbon, best-in-town." With a little juggling, you can change the words to make the song apply to any grade level you want. "A Wee Bit Weird" was written by Stoeri. *(Pr, I)*

Here are more great songs about school:

"Back to School." (Bunny Wailer) Reggae for Kids.

"By the Way." Scruggs, Joe. Deep in the Jungle.

"Cool in School." Harley, Bill. You're in Trouble.

"Day Care Blues." Trout Fishing in America. Big Trouble.

"Do I Have To." Troubadour. On the Trail.

"I've Got a Teacher, She's So Mean." Polisar, Barry Louis. Teacher's Favorites.

"My Name Is Cheech, the School Bus Driver." Marin, Cheech. My Name Is Cheech, the School Bus Driver.

"School Glue." Scruggs, Joe. Abracadabra.

"Trading Lunches." Marin, Cheech. My Name Is Cheech, the School Bus Driver.

"When I Go to School." Parachute Express. Happy to Be Here.

Sickness

"Baby Bear's Chicken Pox." Avni, Fran. Artichokes and Brussel Sprouts.

Ask the children to bring teddy bears. Have them scratch teddy as they listen to this song about a poor little bear who has chicken pox everywhere. Scratch teddy's nose as the bear on the recording cries about his itchy nose. *(Ps)*

"Chicken Pox." Troubadour. On the Trail.

Troubadour sings about spots on the belly, spots on the back, spots and spots everywhere. Make a felt outline of a human. Patterns can be found in *Felt Board Fun* by Liz and

Dick Wilmes. Add little red dots all over it as the song is sung. "Chicken Pox" was written by Judith Steinbergh and Victor Cockburn. **(Ps, Pr)**

"Ebeneezer Sneezer." Penner, Fred. Ebeneezer Sneezer.

Kids get a chance to make the loudest, longest sneeze in musical history. Play the recording after reading the funny, participatory story "Ebeneezer-Never-Could-Sneezer" from Virginia Tashjian's book *With a Deep Sea Smile*. Another fun sneezing song full of sound effects is Paul Tracey's "I Caught a Code" from *The Rainbow Kingdom*. **(Ps, Pr)**

"March of the Germs." Tickle Tune Typhoon. Healthy Beginnings.

Tickle Tune Typhoon sing "The March of the Germs" to the tune of "When Johnny Comes Marching Home." The song describes germs and, in a humorous way, how to prevent them from getting into your body. Share the song with the picture book *Germs Make Me Sick* by Melvin Berger. "March of the Germs" was written by Lorraine Bayes Deardorff and Dennis Westphall. **(Ps, Pr)**

Here are more great songs about being sick:

"Allergies." Penner, Fred. Happy Feet.

"Bellyache." Paxton, Tom. Suzy Is a Rocker.

"Diaper Rash." Polisar, Barry Louis. Family Concert.

"The Flu." Craig 'n Co. Rock 'n Together.

"I Won't Give You My Cold." Gibson, Dee, and Joe Scruggs. Songs to Brighten Your Day.

"I've Got the Measles." Paxton, Tom. Balloon-Alloon-Alloon.

"My Brother Threw Up on My Stuffed Toy Bunny." Polisar, Barry Louis. Family Concert.

"My Brother Threw Up on My Stuffed Toy Bunny." Polisar, Barry Louis. Family Trip.

"No One Knows for Sure." Alsop, Peter. Wha'd'ya Wanna Do?

"Pussy Caught the Measles." Carfra, Pat. Songs for Sleepyheads and Out-of-Beds.

"Too Sick for School." Nagler, Eric. Come On In.

"You Know It Got Better." Ungar, Jay, and Lynn Hardy. A Place to Be.

Spiders

"Anansi." Raffi. Corner Grocery Store.

Play this recording after reading Eric Kimmel's excellent Anansi books *(Anansi and the Moss-Covered Rock, Anansi and the Talking Melon,* and *Anansi Goes Fishing),* all illustrated by Janet Stevens. The calypso beat of Raffi's recording will get the kids so caught up that they'll be singing "Anansi" over and over with the backup singers. "Anansi" was written by Raffi and Bert Simpson. **(Pr)**

* "The Eensy Weensy Spider." Sharon, Lois and Bram. Mainly Mother Goose.

Sharon, Lois and Bram not only sing about the "eensy weensy" spider, but they include verses for the "BIG FAT" spider and the "teensy weensy" spider as well. The trio encourage larger-than-life fingerplay motions for the big spider, and miniscule motions for the teensy one. In his version on *Deep in the Jungle,* Joe Scruggs adds verses in which the spider goes waterskiing, swimming, and dancing. Traditional versions of this song can be found as "The Eensy Weensy Spider" or "The Itsy Bitsy Spider" on:

    Bartels, Joanie. Bathtime Magic.

    Carfra, Pat. Lullabies and Laughter with the Lullaby Lady.

    Dallas, Patti, and Laura Baron. Good Morning Sunshine.

    Monet, Lisa. Circle Time.

    Seeger, Mike and Peggy. American Folk Songs for Children.

Sharon, Lois and Bram. Great Big Hits.
Wee Sing.
Wee Sing around the World.   *(Ps)*

"Spider on the Floor." Raffi. Singable Songs for the Very Young.

Young children can't get enough of this song. Use a spider puppet and have it crawl up your leg, stomach, neck, face, and head. At the end of the song, throw the spider puppet into the crowd shouting "Spider!" This will elicit screams of delight. Just make sure your kids are old enough. (Two- and three-year-olds might cry. I speak from experience.) If you don't have a spider puppet, make your hand crawl up your body like a spider. Or read Raffi's picture book version of the song illustrated by True Kelley. "Spider on the Floor" was written by Bill Russell. "Hey, Mr. Spider" found on Linda Arnold's *Make Believe* and "Hey, Ms. Spider" found on Mary Miché's *Nature Nuts* both feature spiders crawling up people. These last two songs emphasize treating spiders with respect.   *(All)*

"Spider's Web." Diamond, Charlotte. 10 Carrot Diamond.

Diamond has written a gorgeous song about the wonders of spider webs. Read Eric Carle's picture book *A Very Busy Spider.* Afterward, have the children feel the book's textured web while the Diamond recording sets the mood. *(Ps, Pr)*

Teeth

* "Brush Your Teeth." Fink, Cathy. Grandma Slid down the Mountain.

No matter what time you wake up, the best thing to do is brush your teeth!

> *When you wake up in the morning*
> *and it's quarter to one,*
> *You just want to have a little fun,*
> *You brush your teeth.*

Sing this simple song with an oversize toothbrush that you can find in a novelty store (or perhaps from your local dentist). This traditional song can also be found on:

Cassidy, Nancy. Kids' Songs.

Fink, Cathy, and Marcy Marxer. A Cathy and Marcy Collection for Kids.

Raffi. Raffi on Broadway.

Raffi. Singable Songs for the Very Young. **(Ps)**

"Brush Your Teeth (Cepíllense los dientes)." (Fred Miller) Early Ears: Songs Just for 5 Year Olds.

This bilingual tooth song is set to a fast, latino beat. Get the kids up and dancing while they listen to sensible dental habits. Fred Miller sings about brushing at least twice a day and visiting the dentist, in both English and Spanish.

(Ps, Pr)

"Loose Tooth." Troubadour. On the Trail.

The singer is so worried about his loose tooth that he is afraid to chew or even take a deep breath for fear of swallowing the tooth. The children can get up and wiggle like a loose tooth as Troubadour sings "wiggle, wiggle, wiggle" and "jiggle, jiggle, jiggle" during the chorus. This catchy original by Troubadour members Victor Cockburn and Judith Steinbergh is a good companion to the picture book *The Wobbly Tooth* by Nancy Evans Cooney. **(Pr)**

"So Long, You Old Tooth." Brown, Greg. Bathtub Blues.

Brown's very short song compactly describes the frustrations of having a loose tooth that is not willing to go. He is ready to use pliers, tie the tooth to a string and doorknob, bite an apple, even use dynamite. The children can echo sections of the chorus and shout "Yes!" when Brown talks about getting a dollar for the tooth. Brown wrote this song with a class of frustrated, loose-toothed second-graders.

(Pr)

"Tooth Fairy Song." Troubadour. On the Trail.

> This song is told from the Tooth Fairy's point of view. The Tooth Fairy can sneak into your room any number of ways, from skateboarding under the door to flying on a magic carpet. "Tooth Fairy Song" was written by Judith Steinbergh and Victor Cockburn. The song is a great match to the picture book *Tooth Witch* by Barbara Karlin. **(Pr)**

"Toothless." Green Chili Jam Band. Starfishing.

> It is hard to maintain your dignity when milk dribbles out of the space where your teeth are supposed to be. All of the singer's friends wind up wearing his food on their clothes. Kids can echo "toothless" during the chorus. This funny song was written by band members Barney Fuller, Dick Orr, and Ron Torrenz. **(Pr)**

"Up like a Rocket." Whiteley, Ken. All of the Seasons.

> If kids can't remember proper brushing techniques, Whiteley tells them to brush up like a rocket going up, down like the rain falling down, and back and forth like a train going forward and backward on a track. Have the kids follow the proper brushing motions with their fingers as they listen to the recording. "Up like a Rocket" was written by Whiteley and was inspired by his son's dentist. **(Ps, Pr)**

Here are more great songs about teeth:

"Braces." Sprout, Jonathan. On the Radio.

"Brush to the North." Kahn, Si. Good Times and Bed Times.

"Dinosaur Tooth Care." Phipps, Bonnie. Dinosaur Choir.

"I Brush My Teeth." Peanutbutterjam. Peanutbutterjam Goes to School.

"I Sure Have Got a Loose Tooth." Charette, Rick. Bubble Gum and Other Songs for Hungry Kids.

"Little White Star." McCutcheon, John. Family Garden.

"Loose Tooth Blues." Gemini. Growing Up Together.

"Pearly White Waltz." Tickle Tune Typhoon. All of Us Will
Shine.

"Sugar." Rosenshontz. It's the Truth.

"Tooth Fairy." Rosenshontz. Family Vacation.

"Us Kids Brush Our Teeth." Alsop, Peter. Stayin' Over.

Transportation

**"The Choo Choo Song." (Karan and the Musical Medicine
Show) Early Ears: Songs Just for 1 Year Olds.**

Karan and the Musical Medicine Show sing this cumulative
train song filled with sound effects. The children can shout
"choo choo," "all aboard," "ya-hoo," and more. Another
song full of locomotive sound effects is "The Train Song" by
Janice Buckner on both her recordings *Little Friends for Little
Folks* and *All Aboard the Learn Along Train.* **(Ps, Pr)**

**"Flying 'round the Mountain." Scruggs, Joe. Even Trolls
Have Moms.**

Scruggs created a new version of the traditional "She'll Be
Coming 'round the Mountain" complete with helicopters,
jet planes, and motorcycles. Grandmother not only rides all
of the above, but she buys a computer and earns her doc-
torate, too. The kids can hold their arms out for the plane,
twirl them overhead for the helicopter, and "gun" the han-
dlebars of their motorcycles. They can create new verses for
Grandma that shatter all stereotypes of the elderly ("She'll
be taking karate lessons when she comes"). Traditional versions of "She'll Be Coming 'round the Mountain can be
found on:
Cassidy, Nancy. Kids' Songs 2.
Greg and Steve. We All Live Together, Vol. 2.
Little Richard. Shake It All Around.
Rosenthal, Phil. Comin' round the Mountain.
Roth, Kevin, Oscar, Bingo, and Buddies.
Roth, Kevin. Travel Song Sing Alongs.

Seeger, Mike and Peggy. American Folk Songs for
  Children.
Seeger, Pete. Family Concert.
Seeger, Pete. Stories and Songs for Little Children.
Sharon, Lois and Bram. All the Fun You Can Sing!
Sharon, Lois and Bram. Great Big Hits.
Sharon, Lois and Bram. One Elephant, Deux Elephants.
Wee Sing.
Wee Sing Sing-Alongs.   *(All)*

* "Let's Go Riding." Grammer, Red. Can You Sound Just like Me?

Grammer leads the kids on a trip via motorcycle, jet plane,
fire engine, a truck full of 200 pigs, and a horse that won't
budge and then won't stop. There is a step-by-step description of riding in each vehicle and plenty of sound effects.
                                                       (Ps, Pr)

"Little Red Caboose." Wee Sing Fun 'n' Folk.

Wee Sing combines two versions of this traditional song.
This combination would make a wonderful presentation for
a school assembly. In all versions, the children can sing
"chug, chug, chug." Sweet Honey in the Rock's version (list-
ed three times below) is a tour de force that will impress
upon children the power of the human voice. "Little Red
Caboose" can also be found on:
  Bartels, Joanie. Travelin' Magic.
  A Child's Celebration of Song. (Sweet Honey in the
    Rock)
  Family Folk Festival. (Sweet Honey in the Rock)
  Monet, Lisa. Circle Time.
  Sweet Honey in the Rock. All for Freedom.   *(All)*

* "Little Red Wagon." Buchman, Rachel. Hello Everybody.

Buchman gives very specific movement directions in her
variation of this traditional song. The children will be
crawling, wagging their fingers, jumping, walking, jolting,

and falling down. A more traditional version can be found as "Bumping Up and Down" on:

> Raffi. Singable Songs for the Very Young.　　　*(Ps)*

"Long Way Home." Chapin, Tom. Family Tree.

Chapin and his writing partner, John Forster, have written my favorite travel song, which turns into a litany of excuses for why the singer is late for dinner. Children will be inspired to create their own tall tales after hearing this recording. They will also delight in singing, "It was a long, long, long, long, long way home," after each stanza. Share the song with the picture book *A Weekend in the Country* by Lee Lorenz. Some of Lorenz's hilarious travel plans are similar to those found in the song.　　　*(Pr, I)*

"The New Wheels on the Bus." Rappin' Rob.
The Rappin' Rob Rap.

The traditional "Wheels on the Bus" is a longtime storytime favorite. Rappin' Rob adapted the tune and added a sports car, a rocket ship, and a donkey cart complete with sound effects. More traditional versions of "Wheels on the Bus" can be found on:

> Bartels, Joanie. Travelin' Magic.
> Cassidy, Nancy. Kids' Songs 2 (listed on this album as "The Bus Song").
> Monet, Lisa. Circle Time.
> Raffi. Rise and Shine.
> Sharon, Lois and Bram. The Elephant Show Record.
> Weissman, Jackie. Peanut Butter, Tarzan, and Roosters.
> 　　　*(Ps, Pr)*

"Packin' for My Hike." Miché, Mary. Nature Nuts.

As the lyrics say, "It's a simple song that anyone can sing." The singer lists items she is contemplating taking on a camping trip. The children can shout "yes" or "no" for each item she mentions. A first-aid kit? Yes! Video games? No!

　　　(I)

* **"Riding in My Car." Guthrie, Woody. Woody's 20 Grow Big Songs.**

  There are plenty of sound effects in Guthrie's simple, easy-to-learn car song. The children will find themselves click-clacking the door, rattling on the front seat, making a "brrm" engine noise, and blowing the horn with a loud "a-oorah, a-oougah." The song, also known as "Car, Car," can be found on:
  > Bartels, Joanie. Travelin' Magic.
  > Neat, Roxanne, and David Stoeri. Dance, Boatman, Dance.
  > Penner, Fred. Collections.
  > Penner, Fred. Ebeneezer Sneezer. **(All)**

"The Stoplight." Rogers, Sally. What Can One Little Person Do?

Rogers sings about stopping for red and going on green. Make a felt traffic light with interchangeable lights. A pattern can be found in Liz and Dick Wilmes's *Felt Board Fun*. "The Stoplight" was written by Rogers and her daughter Malana. **(Ps, Pr)**

"Trans Canadian Super-Continental Special Express." Penner, Fred. Fred Penner's Place.

Here is another tongue-twisting phrase the children will enjoy learning. In addition to singing the title over and over, there are plenty of "whoo-whoo," "chugga-chugga," and other train sounds. "Trans Canadian Super-Continental Special Express" was written by Penner and Sheldon Oberman. **(Pr, I)**

Here are more great transportation songs:

"All Aboard." Lonnquist, Ken. Welcome 2 Kenland.

"Almost Home." Scruggs, Joe. Bahamas Pajamas.

"Are We There Yet?" Craig 'n Co. Rock 'n Toontown.

"Are We There Yet?" Scruggs, Joe. Traffic Jams.

"The Awful Hilly Daddy-Willie Trip." (John McCutcheon) Grandma's Patchwork Quilt.

"The Awful Hilly Daddy-Willie Trip." McCutcheon, John. Mail Myself to You.

"Beep Beep." Bartels, Joanie. Travelin' Magic.

"Bicycle." Parachute Express. Shakin' It!

"Big Toe Truck." Scruggs, Joe. Traffic Jams.

"Buckle Up." Scruggs, Joe. Traffic Jams.

"Choo-Choo." Parachute Express. Shakin' It!

"Down by the Station." Carfra, Pat. Lullabies and Laughter with the Lullaby Lady.

"Down by the Station." Dallas, Patti, and Laura Baron. Playtime Parade.

"Down by the Station." Wee Sing.

"Down by the Station." Wee Sing Sing-Alongs.

"Down the Railroad Track." Lonnquist, Ken. Welcome 2 Kenland.

"Family Vacation." Rosenshontz. Family Vacation.

"Fantasy Automobile." Parachute Express. Sunny Side Up.

"Freight Train." Garcia, Jerry, and David Grissman. Not for Kids Only.

"Freight Train." Seeger, Pete. Family Concert.

"Get on My Bike." Charette, Rick. Chickens on Vacation.

"The Happy Wanderer." Staines, Bill. The Happy Wanderer.

"It's My Mother and My Father and My Sister and the Dog." Polisar, Barry Louis. Family Trip.

"Late Night Radio." Brown, Greg. Bathtub Blues.

"The Little Engine That Could." Ives, Burl. Little White Duck.

"Little Red Car." Schneider, Bob. Listen to the Children.

"Mingulay Boat Song." Grammer, Red. Red Grammer's Favorite Sing Along Songs.

"New Car." McCutcheon, John. Mail Myself to You.

"New River Train." Fink, Cathy. Grandma Slid down the Mountain.

"New River Train." Raffi. More Singable Songs.

"On the Trail." Troubadour. On the Trail.

"One Speed Bike." Lonnquist, Ken. Welcome 2 Kenland.

"The People in the Car." Scruggs, Joe. Traffic Jams.

"Places in the World." Grammer, Red. Teaching Peace.

"Pufferbellies." Sharon, Lois and Bram. All the Fun You Can Sing!

"Pufferbellies." Sharon, Lois and Bram. Great Big Hits.

"Pufferbellies." Sharon, Lois and Bram. In the Schoolyard.

"Pufferbellies." Sharon, Lois and Bram. One, Two, Three, Four, Live!

"Sailing to the Sea." Chapin, Tom. Mother Earth.

"Take Me with You." Alsop, Peter. Take Me with You.

"What Will I Take to the Moon?" Parachute Express. Happy to Be Here.

Weather

"Great High Wind." Nagler, Eric. Come On In.

The wind blew so hard it wrinkled the skin of an alligator and played a tune on the church organ. Direct the children to make great big blowing noises while they listen to this bluegrass fiddle tune. Read *Iva Dunnit and the Big Wind* written by Carol Purdy and illustrated by Steven Kellogg. Iva Dunnit has to contend with a big wind that threatens to blow away her best layin' chickens. **(Pr, I)**

"I Am the Wind." Penner, Fred. Fred Penner's Place.

This song is my favorite Penner original. It is beautifully melodic and has what sounds like pan flutes or South American flutes accenting the song. Encourage the children to act out the motion of wind while listening to the recording. **(Pr)**

**"It Snowed Last Night." Baron, Laura, and Patti Dallas.
Songs for the Earth.**

What fun children have when they see the first snowfall.
The song soon breaks into "I'm a Little Snowman" to the
tune of "I'm a Little Teapot." Have the children act out the
motions and "melt" by sliding down to the floor. Several
fine companion picture books come to mind, most notably
First Snowfall by Anne and Harlow Rockwell, *The Jacket I
Wear in the Snow* by Shirley Neitzel, and *Froggy Gets Dressed*
by Jonathan London.   *(Ps, Pr)*

**"Mushroom Umbrellas." Walker, Mary Lu.
The Frog's Party.**

A hoppy toad, a bumblebee, and the singer all huddle
underneath a mushroom to escape the rain. The song is a
natural companion to the picture book *Mushroom in the
Rain* by Mirra Ginsburg and illustrated by Jose Aruego and
Ariane Dewey. "Mushroom Umbrellas" was written by
Walker.   *(Ps, Pr)*

**"The Puddle Song." (Karan and the Musical Medicine
Show) Early Ears: Songs Just for 2 Year Olds.**

Make twenty-five little teardrop-shaped felt raindrops. They
in turn change into one, two . . . twenty-five puddles on the
ground. Make either twenty-five small felt puddles, or group
the twenty-five raindrops into one large puddle. The song
was written by Karan Bunin Huss.   *(Ps)*

"Puddles." Diamond, Charlotte. My Bear Gruff.

Diamond's original call-and-response song is all about playing in the rain. Boots go smacking, tongues catch raindrops,
and everyone hops like a frog while splashing in the puddles. The song ends with the appearance of a rainbow. *(Ps)*

"The Rain Round." Rogers, Sally. Piggyback Planet.

This song is a great challenge for a music class. The steps of
the water cycle are repeated over and over, just as a round
is repeated over and over. The rain falls down, flows to the

sea as rivers, and is gathered back up by the clouds. Lots of drip-a-drop-a-drip-a-drops. "The Rain Round" was written by Rogers.   *(I)*

"Rainwater." Scooter. Calling All Kids.

The background chorus and sound effects of this pretty song make you feel like the rain is falling all around you. Play this recording while showing Peter Spier's wordless picture book *Rain* (especially on a rainy day). "Rainwater" was written by Jim Kimball.   *(Ps, Pr)*

"The Thunder Song." Monet, Lisa. My Best Friend.

This very short clapping song is full of thunderstorm effects. Claps make the thunder, lightning is simulated by the children splaying their hands in the air, and splashes are made by slapping the ground. When Monet sings "down, down, down," move your fingers as if rain was falling. "The Thunder Song" was written by Vickie Neville.   *(Ps)*

* "What You Gonna Wear?" Fink, Cathy, and Marcy Marxer. Help Yourself.

What are you going to wear when it's raining, snowing, hot, or cool outside? The children will respond with the correct answers. Make felt cutouts of a raincoat, winter coat, hat, mittens, sweater, and shorts to cue their answers. Patterns for all of these can be found in *Felt Board Fun* by Liz and Dick Wilmes. "What You Gonna Wear?" was written by Marxer.
                                                                  (Ps, Pr)

Here are more great songs about weather:

"Ain't Gonna Rain/Rain, Rain, Go Away." Greg and Steve. Playing Favorites.

"Andy's Little Umbrella." McCornack, Mike and Carleen. Beasties, Bumbershoots, and Lullabies.

"Another Rainy Day." Rory. I'm Just a Kid.

"I Like to Be Cold and Wet." Troubadour. On the Trail.

"It Ain't Gonna Rain No More." Penner, Fred. The Cat Came Back.

"It Ain't Gonna Rain No More." Roth, Kevin. Oscar, Bingo, and Buddies.

"It Rained a Mist." Seeger, Mike and Peggy. American Folk Songs for Children.

"It's a Rainy Day." Charette, Rick. Alligator in the Elevator.

"It's Raining." Peter, Paul and Mary. Peter, Paul and Mommy.

"Let the Wild Wind Blow." Paxton, Tom. Suzy Is a Rocker.

"Listen to the Raindrops." Schneider, Bob. Listen to the Children.

"Pray for Snow." Gemini. Growing Up Together.

"Raining Cats and Dogs." Foote, Norman. Foote Prints.

"Rainy Day." Block, Cathy. Timeless.

"Shoveling." Chapin, Tom. Family Tree.

"Snow Song." Walker, Mary Lu. The Frog's Party.

"Snowing." Sprout, Jonathan. On the Radio.

"Snowman." Rosenshontz. Family Vacation.

"So Cold Outside." Avni, Fran. Artichokes and Brussel Sprouts.

"Water Cycle Boogie." Banana Slug String Band. Slugs at Sea.

"Weather Song." Gibson, Dee, and Joe Scruggs. Songs to Brighten Your Day.

"What Do You Do on a Rainy Day?" Rosen, Gary. Tot Rock.

"What Have They Done to the Rain?" Rogers, Sally. Piggyback Planet.

"Who Has Seen the Wind?" Buchman, Rachel. Hello Rachel! Hello Children!

"Wind." Avni, Fran. Artichokes and Brussel Sprouts.

"The Wind and the Rain." Dallas, Patti, and Laura Baron. Good Morning Sunshine.

Short Takes

Select listings of other popular storytime and classroom themes.

Cowboys/Cowgirls

"Cowboy's Lament." Penner, Fred. A House for Me.

"The Desperado." Cassidy, Nancy. Kids' Songs 2.

"Ghost Riders in the Sky." Bishop, Heather. Purple People Eater.

"Ghost Riders in the Sky." Cassidy, Nancy. Kids' Songs 2.

"Ghost Riders in the Sky." Penner, Fred. The Cat Came Back.

"Ghost Riders in the Sky." Penner, Fred. Collections.

"I'd Like to Be a Cowgirl." Fink, Cathy. Grandma Slid down the Mountain.

"Long Tall Texan." Bishop, Heather. Bellybutton.

"The Old Chisholm Trail." Cassidy, Nancy. Kids' Songs 2.

"The Old Chisholm Trail." Penner, Fred. Ebeneezer Sneezer.

"Ol' Texas." Cassidy, Nancy. Kids' Songs 2.

"Old Texas." Sharon, Lois and Bram. One, Two, Three, Four, Live!

"Ride 'Em High/The Cowpoke Dance." Marxer, Marcy. Jump Children.

"Riding Along (Singing a Cowboy Song)." Sharon, Lois and Bram. Smorgasbord.

"Rockabye Ranch." Atkinson, Lisa. The One and Only Me.

"The Trail Ride." Chapin, Tom. Moonboat.

"Under the Stars." Cappelli, Frank. Pass the Coconut.

Earth

"Big Beautiful Planet." Raffi. Evergreen, Everblue.

"Big Beautiful Planet." Raffi. Raffi on Broadway.

"Big Beautiful Planet." Raffi. Rise and Shine.

"Big Beautiful Planet." Whiteley, Ken. All of the Seasons.

"Big Big World." Harley, Bill. Big Big World.

"Chant for the Earth." The Van Manens. Healthy Planet, Healthy People.

"The Earth Is Our Home." Baron, Laura, and Patti Dallas. Songs for the Earth.

"Earth Is Our Home." Kinnoin, Dave. Daring Dewey.

"Earthkeeper." The Van Manens. We Recycle.

"Evergreen, Everblue." Raffi. Evergreen, Everblue.

"Evergreen, Everblue." Raffi. Raffi on Broadway.

"Happy Earth Day." Chapin, Tom. Billy the Squid.

"Hug the Earth." (Tickle Tune Typhoon) Peace Is the World Smiling.

"Hug the Earth." Tickle Tune Typhoon. Hug the Earth.

"K'ang Ting Song." Rogers, Sally. Piggyback Planet.

"K.S.E. Promise Song." Raffi. Raffi on Broadway.

"Living on a Planet I Love." Parachute Express. Over Easy.

"Magical Earth." Pirtle, Sarah. Magical Earth.

"Mother Earth's Routine." Chapin, Tom. Mother Earth.

"One Earth." Shontz, Bill. Animal Tales.

"Our Dear, Dear Mother." Raffi. Evergreen, Everblue.

"Our Dear Mother Earth." Baron, Laura, and Patti Dallas. Songs for the Earth.

"Pretty Planet." Chapin, Tom. Family Tree.

"This Is Our World." Baron, Laura, and Patti Dallas. Songs for the Earth.

"This Land Is Your Land." Rogers, Sally. Piggyback Planet.

"La tierra es mi madre." Rogers, Sally. Piggyback Planet.

"Two Hands Hold the Earth." Pirtle, Sarah. Two Hands Hold the Earth.

"Up in Space." Walker, Mary Lu. The Frog's Party.

"Walkin' around the Sun." Pease, Tom. Wobbi-Do-Wop.

"What Can We Do to Save Our Planet?" Janet and Judy. Musical Almanac.

Fish

"At the Codfish Ball." Bethie. Bethie's Really Silly Songs about Animals.

"At the Codfish Ball." The Chenille Sisters. 1-2-3 for Kids.

"At the Codfish Ball." Penner, Fred. Happy Feet.

"At the 'Quarium." Paxton, Tom. Balloon-Alloon-Alloon.

"Billy the Squid." Chapin, Tom. Billy the Squid.

"Bubble the Fish." Avni, Fran. Daisies and Ducklings.

"Can You Show Us?" Parachute Express. Sunny Side Up.

"Crawdad." Penner, Fred. A House for Me.

"The Crawdad Song." Watson, Doc. Doc Watson Sings Songs for Little Pickers.

"Crawdad Song." Wee Sing Fun 'n' Folk.

"The Dancing Fish." Buckner, Janice. All Aboard the Learn Along Train.

"Fish Are Orderly." Paxton, Tom. Balloon-Alloon-Alloon.

"The Fishin' Hole." Penner, Fred. Fred Penner's Place.

"Goin' Fishin'." Rosenshontz. Family Vacation.

"The Goldfish Bowl." Avni, Fran. Daisies and Ducklings.

"Jaws." Colleen and Uncle Squaty. Colleen and Uncle Squaty.

"Jump, Salmon, Jump." Pirtle, Sarah. Two Hands Hold the Earth.

"Little Fish." Cassidy, Nancy. Kids' Songs Sleepyheads.

"Night Caps." Carfra, Pat. Babes, Beasts, and Birds.

"Octopus." Diamond, Charlotte. 10 Carrot Diamond.

"Les Petites Poissons." Sharon, Lois and Bram. Sing A to Z.

"Three Little Fishes." Sharon, Lois and Bram. Mainly Mother Goose.

"Three Little Fishies." Bartels, Joanie. Bathtime Magic.

Occupations

"I Can Be Most Anything I Try." Charette, Rick. Alligator in the Elevator.

"Nobody Sings at Work Today." Rockow, Corrine. I Sing Every Day of My Life.

"What a Day!" Craig 'n Co. Morning 'n Night.

"What Does Your Mama Do?" Fink, Cathy. Grandma Slid down the Mountain.

"What Does Your Mama Do?" Pease, Tom. Boogie Boogie Boogie.

"What Does Your Mama Do?" Winter, Cathy, and Betsy Rose. As Strong as Anyone Can Be.

"When I Get Big." Jennings, Waylon. Cowboys, Sisters, Rascals, and Dirt.

"When I Grow Up." The Chenille Sisters. The Big Picture.

"When I Grow Up." Harley, Bill. Monsters in the Bathroom.

Outer Space

"93 Million Miles Away." Janet and Judy. Musical Almanac.

"Constellations." Livingston, Bob. Open the Window.

"The Galaxy Song." Sharon, Lois and Bram. Stay Tuned.

"Hold That Moon." Block, Cathy. Timeless.

"I'd Like to Live on the Moon." The Chenille Sisters. 1-2-3 for Kids.

"The Man Who Ran Away with the Moon." Foote, Norman. If the Shoe Fits.

"Mister Sun." Cassidy, Nancy. Kids' Songs.

"Mister Sun." Sharon, Lois and Bram. Sing A to Z.

"The Moon Song." Penner, Fred. What a Day!

"Moonboat." Chapin, Tom. Moonboat.

"Mr. Spaceman." Harley, Bill. 50 Ways to Fool Your Mother.

"Mr. Sun." Raffi. Singable Songs for the Very Young.

"Mr. Sun, Sun." Roth, Kevin. Dinosaurs, Dragons, and Other Children's Songs.

"Nine Planets." Janet and Judy. Musical Almanac.

"One Light, One Sun." Raffi. Evergreen, Everblue.

"One Light, One Sun." Raffi. One Light, One Sun.

"One Light, One Sun." Raffi. Raffi in Concert with the Rise and Shine Band.

"One Light, One Sun." Raffi. Raffi on Broadway.

"Star Sun." Scruggs, Joe. Bahamas Pajamas.

"The Stars Are Coming Out like Popcorn." Pease, Tom. Wobbi-Do-Wop.

"Sun, Sun." McCornack, Mike and Carleen. Sunshine Cake.

"Twinkle, Twinkle, Little Star." Cassidy, Nancy. Kids' Songs.

"Twinkle, Twinkle, Little Star." Herdman, Priscilla. Stardreamer.

"Twinkle, Twinkle, Little Star." Little Richard. Shake It All About.

"Twinkle, Twinkle, Little Star." McCornack, Mike and Carleen. Beasties, Bumbershoots, and Lullabies.

"Twinkle, Twinkle, Little Star." Raffi. One Light, One Sun.

"Twinkle, Twinkle, Little Star." Sharon, Lois and Bram. One Elephant, Deux Elephants.

"Twinkle, Twinkle, Little Star." Tickle Tune Typhoon. All of Us Will Shine.

"What Will I Take to the Moon?" Parachute Express. Happy to Be Here.

Peace

"Across the Wide Ocean." Pirtle, Sarah. Two Hands Hold the Earth.

"Chickens for Peace." Alsop, Peter. Take Me with You.

"Chickens for Peace." Miché, Mary. Peace It Together.

"Dear Mr. President." Alsop, Peter. Stayin' Over.

"Find a Peaceful Thought." Arnold, Linda. Make Believe.

"Find a Peaceful Thought." Miché, Mary. Peace It Together.

"Find a Peaceful Thought." (Linda Arnold) Peace Is the World Smiling."

"Kids' Peace Song." Alsop, Peter. Take Me with You.

"Kids' Peace Song." Miché, Mary. Peace It Together.

"Kids' Peace Song." (Peter Alsop) Peace Is the World Smiling.

"Let There Be Peace on Earth." Miché, Mary. Peace It Together.

"Let's Live Peacefully." Arnold, Linda. Peppermint Wings.

"A Little Peace Song." Walker, Mary Lu. The Frog's Party.

"Mir, Peace." Miché, Mary. Peace It Together.

"One Earth." Arnold, Linda. Happiness Cake.

"P Is for Peace." Rogers, Sally. What Can One Little Person Do?

"Paz y libertad." Pirtle, Sarah. Magical Earth.

"Peace and Love." (Peter Broggs) Reggae for Kids.

"Peace Is the World Smiling." (Children of Selma) Peace Is the World Smiling.

"Peace Round." Pease, Tom. Boogie Boogie Boogie.

"Silly Old Peace Song." Miché, Mary. Peace It Together.

"Song of Peace." Miché, Mary. Peace It Together.

"The Strangest Dream." Nagler, Eric. Improvise with Eric Nagler.

"Teaching Peace." Grammer, Red. Teaching Peace.

"There Is a Fine Wind Blowing." Tickle Tune Typhoon. All of Us Will Shine.

"Unite Children." Rainbow Song.

"Use a Word." Grammer, Red. Teaching Peace.

"Use a Word." Miché, Mary. Peace It Together.

"What Is Peace?" The Van Manens. We Recycle.

"With Two Wings." Grammer, Red. Teaching Peace.

"Yambo." Crow, Dan. Oops!

"Yambo." Miché, Mary. Peace It Together.

Reading

"Come Read a Book." Palmer, Hap. Babysong.

"Good Night Story Time." Palmer, Hap. Peek-a-Boo.

"I Found It in a Book." Tracey, Paul. The Rainbow Kingdom.

"I Like Reading." Charette, Rick. Where Do My Sneakers Go at Night?

"I'm a Book." Foote, Norman. Foote Prints.

"Just One More Book." Pease, Tom. Wobbi-Do-Wop.

"The Messed-Up Rap." Rappin' Rob. The Rappin' Rob Rap.

"The Rappin' Rob Rap." Rappin' Rob. The Rappin' Rob Rap.

"Read a Book." Arnold, Linda. Peppermint Wings.

"Read a Book." Fink, Cathy, and Marcy Marxer. Help Yourself.

"Read a Book." Scruggs, Joe. Deep in the Jungle.

"Read a Book to Me." Pease, Tom. I'm Gonna Reach.

"Read to Me." The Chenille Sisters. The Big Picture.

"Two Books." Diamond, Charlotte. My Bear Gruff.

Safety

"Buckle Up." Scruggs, Joe. Traffic Jams.

"Irish Seatbelt Jig." Alsop, Peter. Take Me with You.

"The Name and Address Song." Fink, Cathy, and Marcy Marxer. Help Yourself.

"Never Talk to Strangers." Fink, Cathy, and Marcy Marxer. Help Yourself.

"Safety Break." Greg and Steve. Kidding Around.

"Speed Bump Blues." Scruggs, Joe. Traffic Jams.

"Star Sun." Scruggs, Joe. Bahamas Pajamas.

"Stop, Look, and Listen." Fink, Cathy, and Marcy Marxer. Help Yourself.

"Stop, Look, and Listen." Monet, Lisa. My Best Friend.

"The Stoplight." Rogers, Sally. What Can One Little Person Do?

"Thinking Safety." Tickle Tune Typhoon. Healthy Beginnings.

Seasons

"All of the Seasons." Whiteley, Ken. All of the Seasons.

"Autumn Song." Baron, Laura, and Patti Dallas. Songs for the Earth.

"Autumn Winds." McCornack, Mike and Carleen. Sunshine Cake.

"Family Garden." McCutcheon, John. Family Garden.

"Footprints." Rory. Make-Believe Day.

"Four Seasons." Baron, Laura, and Patti Dallas. Songs for the Earth.

"Hello Winter." Diamond, Charlotte. Diamonds and Dragons.

"I Can't Wait for Spring." Pirtle, Sarah. The Wind Is Telling Secrets.

"I Can't Wait for Spring." Whiteley, Ken. All of the Seasons.

"Jumping in the Leaves." Nagler, Eric. Improvise with Eric Nagler.

"Late on a Cold Winter Night." Rosenthal, Phil. Comin' round the Mountain.

"Mother Earth's Routine." Chapin, Tom. Mother Earth.

"Pumpkin Town." Pirtle, Sarah. The Wind Is Telling Secrets.

"Seasons." Avni, Fran. Daisies and Ducklings.

"So Cold Outside." Avni, Fran. Artichokes and Brussel Sprouts.

"Spring Is in the Air." Schneider, Bob. Listen to the Children.

"Summer Time, Winter Time." Colleen and Uncle Squaty. Colleen and Uncle Squaty.

"Sunshine Summertime." Baron, Laura, and Patti Dallas. Songs for the Earth.

Self-Concept

"The ABC's of You." Grammer, Red. Down the Do-Re-Mi.

"The ABC's of You." Penner, Fred. What a Day!

"Alive and Dreaming." Raffi. Evergreen, Everblue.

"All of Us Will Shine." Tickle Tune Typhoon. All of Us Will Shine.

"Aren't You Glad You're You." Feinstein, Michael. Pure Imagination.

"Believe in Yourself." Greg and Steve. Kidding Around.

"The Best That I Can." Rosenshontz. Rock 'n' Roll Teddy Bear.

"The Bump." Penner, Fred. Collections.

"The Bump." Penner, Fred. Poco.

"Different Drum." Scruggs, Joe. Ants.

"Each of Us Is a Flower." Diamond, Charlotte. 10 Carrot Diamond.

"Everybody Is Somebody." (Taj Mahal) Peace Is the World Smiling.

"Everyone Is Differently Abled." Tickle Tune Typhoon. All of Us Will Shine.

"Express Yourself." Vitamin L. Singin' in the Key of L.

"Grow in Your Own Sweet Way." Chapin, Tom. Moonboat.

"He Eats Asparagus." Alsop, Peter. Take Me with You.

"Healthy Planet, Healthy People." The Van Manens. Healthy Planet, Healthy People.

"Help Yourself." Fink, Cathy, and Marcy Marxer. Help Yourself.

"I Am a Person." Pirtle, Sarah. Two Hands Hold the Earth.

"I Believe in Me." Tickle Tune Typhoon. Hearts and Hands.

"I Believe in Myself." Fink, Cathy, and Marcy Marxer. Help Yourself.

"I Can Be Most Anything I Try." Charette, Rick. Alligator in the Elevator.

"I Can Be Somebody." Buckner, Janice. Everybody's Special.

"I Can Do Anything." Noah, Tim. In Search of the Wow Wow Wibble Woggle Wazzie Woodle Woo!

"I Can Do That." Parachute Express. Sunny Side Up.

"I Think You're Wonderful." Grammer, Red. Teaching Peace.

"I'm a Little Cookie." (Larry Penn) Grandma's Patchwork Quilt.

"I'm a Little Cookie." McCutcheon, John. Mail Myself to You.

"I'm a Little Cookie." Pease, Tom. Boogie Boogie Boogie.

"I'm Just Me." Bennett, Glenn. I Must Be Growing.

"Inside." Peter, Paul and Mary. Peter, Paul and Mommy, Too.

"It's Great Being Me." Penner, Fred. What a Day!

"Let 'Em Laugh." Alsop, Peter. Take Me with You.

"Listen to the Children." Schneider, Bob. Listen to the Children.

"Little Cookie." Alsop, Peter. Take Me with You.

"Love Me for Who I Am." Diamond, Charlotte. 10 Carrot Diamond.

"My Very Own Frame." Vitamin L. Singin' in the Key of L.

"Nobody Else like Me." Fink, Cathy, and Marcy Marxer. Help Yourself.

"Nobody Else like Me." Walker, Mary Lu. The Frog's Party.

"Oh, What a Miracle." Palmer, Hap. Peek-a-Boo.

"The One and Only Me." Atkinson, Lisa. The One and Only Me.

"Proud." Penner, Fred. Happy Feet.

"See Me Beautiful." Grammer, Red. Teaching Peace.

"Shine Out." Tickle Tune Typhoon. Hearts and Hands.

"Think for Yourself." Vitamin L. Walk a Mile.

"This Little Light." Dallas, Patti, and Laura Baron. Playtime Parade.

"This Little Light." Pease, Tom. I'm Gonna Reach.

"This Little Light of Mine." Cassidy, Nancy. Kids' Songs.

"This Little Light of Mine." Gemini. Growing Up Together.

"This Little Light of Mine." Raffi. Raffi in Concert with the Rise and Shine Band.

"This Little Light of Mine." Raffi. Raffi on Broadway.

"This Little Light of Mine." Raffi. Rise and Shine.

"This Little Light of Mine." Rainbow Sign.

"Who Could Possibly Ask for More?" Foote, Norman. If the Shoe Fits.

"Who's Good?" Kinnoin, David. Fun-a-Rooey.

"With These Hands." Vitamin L. Singin' in the Key of L.

"You Are You." Roth, Kevin. Unbearable Bears.

"You Can Be a Giant." Atkinson, Lisa. I Wanna Tickle the Fish.

"You'll Come Shining Through." Chapin, Tom. Moonboat.

"You're Okay!" Alsop, Peter. Stayin' Over.

Sports

"At the Dinosaur Baseball Game." Arnold, Linda. Peppermint Wings.

"The Baseball Kids." Paxton, Tom. Suzy Is a Rocker.

"Baseball on the Block." McCutcheon, John. Family Garden.

"The Bowling Song." Raffi. One Light, One Sun.

"The Bowling Song." Raffi. Raffi on Broadway.

"Chicken Wings." Scruggs, Joe. Even Trolls Have Moms.

"I Caught It (The Baseball Song)." Charette, Rick. Chickens on Vacation.

"The Monkeys' Baseball Game." Paxton, Tom. Balloon-Alloon-Alloon.

"Playing Right Field." Roth, Kevin. Daddysongs.

"Right Field." Gemini. Growing Up Together.

"Right Field." Peter, Paul and Mary. Peter, Paul and Mommy, Too.

"Roller Skating." Penner, Fred. Collections.

"Roller Skating." Penner, Fred. Poco.

"Seven Silly Squirrels." Avni, Fran. Daisies and Ducklings.

"Skateboard." Scruggs, Joe. Deep in the Jungle.

"Suzy Is a Rocker." Paxton, Tom. Suzy Is a Rocker.

"Take Me Out to the Ballgame." Raffi. One Light, One Sun.

"Take Me Out to the Ballgame." Sharon, Lois and Bram. The Elephant Show Record.

Toys

"Angela Bundy." McCornack, Mike and Carleen. Sunshine Cake.

"Balloon-Alloon-Alloon." Paxton, Tom. Balloon-Alloon-Alloon.

"Doll and Pet Parade." Wozniak, Doug. Hugs and Kisses.

"I've Got a YoYo." Paxton, Tom. Suzy Is a Rocker.

"The Little Engine That Could." Ives, Burl. Little White Duck.

"The Marvellous Toy." Abell, Timmy. Play All Day.

"The Marvellous Toy." Atkinson, Lisa. I Wanna Tickle the Fish.

"The Marvellous Toy." Carfra, Pat. Lullabies and Laughter with the Lullaby Lady.

"The Marvellous Toy." Paxton, Tom. The Marvellous Toy.

"The Marvellous Toy." Penner, Fred. Ebeneezer Sneezer.

"The Marvelous Toy." McCornack, Mike and Carleen. Beasties, Bumbershoots, and Lullabies.

"Marvelous Toy." Penner, Fred. Collections.

"The Marvelous Toy." Peter, Paul and Mary. Peter, Paul and Mommy.

"Me and My Teddy Bear." Carfra, Pat. Songs for Sleepyheads and Out-of-Beds.

"My Bear." Troubadour. Can We Go Now?

"My Bear Gruff." Diamond, Charlotte. My Bear Gruff.

"My Dolly." Guthrie, Woody. Woody's 20 Grow Big Songs.

"My Dreydel." Raffi. Singable Songs for the Very Young.

"Ode to Toy." Wellington, Bill. WOOF Hits Home.

"Ode to Toy." Wellington, Bill. WOOF's Greatest Bits.

"Raggedy Rag Doll Friend." Palmer, Hap. Peek-a-Boo.

"Rubber Blubber Whale." Diamond, Charlotte. Diamonds and Dragons.

"Rubber Blubber Whale." McCutcheon, John. Howjadoo.

"Share." Palmer, Hap. Babysong.

"The Talking Toy Box." Scruggs, Joe. Even Trolls Have Moms.

"Teddy Bear Hug." Raffi. Everything Grows.

"Teddy Bear King." Arnold, Linda. Peppermint Wings.

"Teddy Bears' Picnic." Atkinson, Lisa. The One and Only Me.

"Teddy Bears' Picnic." Feinstein, Michael. Pure Imagination.

"Teddy Bears' Picnic." Garcia, Jerry, and David Grissman. Not for Kids Only.

"Teddy Bears' Picnic." McCornack, Mike and Carleen. Beasties, Bumbershoots, and Lullabies.

"Teddy Bears' Picnic." Rosenshontz. Rosenshontz Tickles You.

"Teddy Bears' Picnic." Roth, Kevin. Travel Song Sing Alongs.

"Teddy Bears' Picnic." Roth, Kevin. Unbearable Bears.

"Teddy Bears' Picnic." Whiteley, Ken. All of the Seasons.

"Toys." Rory. Make-Believe Day.

Goodbye Songs

A ritual closing song is an effective way to bring a session to an end.

"Don't Say Goodbye." Nagler, Eric. Come On In.

> Nagler warns the listener not to mispronounce the variations of the word "goodbye." Don't say "our feet are sore" for the German "auf wiedersehen," or "reservoir" for the French "au revoir." The song has a wonderful bike horn and percussion solo.   ***(Pr, I)***

"Good-Bye Song." Grunsky, Jack. Children of the Morning.

> Grunsky sings this pretty goodbye song with the help of several children who say goodbye in different languages. "Good-Bye Song" was written by Grunsky.   ***(All)***

Key: Ps: Preschool, 2–5; Pr: Primary, 6–8; I: Intermediate, 9–12;
    *: Simple tunes

"I'm Looking." Gibson, Dee, and Joe Scruggs. Songs to Brighten Your Day.

The singer dismisses her audience by the color of their clothes. For example, all children wearing orange may leave first. Think of other variations to dismiss your kids using this same tune. Try it by hair color or first intitials. "I'm Looking" was written by Dee Gibson. *(Ps, Pr)*

"Sabunana Kusasa." Pease, Tom. Boogie Boogie Boogie.

This beautiful call-and-response song is sung in Zulu. The title phrase means "we will meet tomorrow." Kids will quickly learn the words because of Pease's echo presentation. This traditional Zulu song was adapted by Jerry Brodey. Another African goodbye song is Gemini's "Quaharay" from *Two of a Kind*. "Quaharay," translated by Gemini member Laszlo Slomovitas, is Swahili for "goodbye now." *(All)*

"The Song That Doesn't End." Lewis, Shari. Lamb Chop's Sing-Along, Play-Along.

Many children are familiar with Shari Lewis's television show. Each episode ends with this hilarious song that repeats itself over and over. You can make it a two-minute closer or a twenty-minute closing song (heaven forbid). It reminds me a little of "100 Bottles of Beer on the Wall" the way it can entertain children long past an adult's endurance. "The Song That Doesn't End" was written by Norman Martin. *(Ps, Pr)*

"Wave Goodbye." Rappin' Rob. The Rappin' Rob Rap.

Wave high,	(Wave your hand overhead.)
Wave low,	(Wave your hand by the ground.)
I think it's time,	(Point to your wrist.)
We've gotta go.	(Point to the door.)
Wave your elbows,	(Flap your elbows.)
Wave your toes,	(Wiggle your toes.)

Wave your tongue	(Wave your tongue.)
And wave your nose.	(Wrinkle your nose.)
Wave your knees,	(Shake your knees.)
Wave your lips,	(Move your lips.)
Blow a kiss	(Pucker up.)
With fingertips.	(Blow a kiss with your fingers.)
Wave your ears,	(Move your ears.)
Wave your hair,	(Shake your hair.)
Wave your belly	(Shake your belly.)
And derriere.	(Shake your hips.)
Wave your chin,	(Move your chin.)
Wave your eye,	(Wink.)
Wave your hand	(Wave your hand.)
And say, "Goodbye!"	

This "Wave Goodbye" rap was written by Rob Reid.   *(All)*

Here are more great goodbye songs:

"Bye Bye." Gemini. Growing Up Together.
"Bye-Bye Pizza Pie." Parachute Express. Sunny Side Up.
"Bye Bye Song." Lonnquist, Ken. Welcome 2 Kenland.
"Going Away." Rosenshontz. Share It.
"Goodbye." Greg and Steve. We All Live Together, Vol. 1.
"Goodbye Everybody." Buchman, Rachel. Hello Rachel! Hello
    Children!
"Goodbye Waltz." Whiteley, Ken. All of the Seasons.
"Happy Trails." Fink, Cathy. When the Rain Comes Down.
"It's Been a Big Day." Foote, Norman. If the Shoe Fits.
"Meetin' in the Building." Sharon, Lois and Bram. In the
    Schoolyard.
"Meeting at the Building." Sweet Honey in the Rock. All for
    Freedom.

"Now the Day Is Over." Wee Sing Sing-Alongs.

"So Long." Harley, Bill. Big Big World.

"Together Tomorrow." Chapin, Tom. Family Tree.

"When I Went Out." Avni, Fran. Artichokes and Brussel Sprouts.

Songs Listed by Special Type

Call-and-Response Songs

Call-and-response songs (or echo songs) are fun in programs or classrooms regardless of the topic. Children repeat each line that they hear, or either parts of a song, or the entire song. Or the leader might teach a specific response, such as saying "Yes, ma'am" after each line. The American folk song "Oh, John the Rabbit" is an example of the latter.

Leader:	Oh, John the rabbit."
Children:	"Yes, ma'am."
Leader:	"Had a mighty bad habit."
Children:	"Yes, ma'am."
Leader:	"Jumping in my garden."
Children:	"Yes, ma'am."
Leader:	"Stealing all the carrots."
Children:	"Yes, ma'am."

Here is a list of great call-and-response songs:

"Ain't Got It No More." Drake, David HB. Kid-Stuff.

"All Hid." Sharon, Lois and Bram. Singing 'n Swinging.

"Bathtub Blues." Brown, Greg. Bathtub Blues.

"The Bear." Wee Sing Fun 'n' Folk.

"The Beat." LaFond, Lois. I Am Who I Am!

"The Best Old Hat." Peanutbutterjam. Simply Singable.

"Big Green Monster." Nagler, Eric. Come On In.

"Bill Grogan's Goat." Wee Sing Silly Songs.

"Bling Blang." Rockow, Corrine. I Sing Every Day of My Life.

"Cadima." Jenkins, Ella. You'll Sing a Song and I'll Sing a Song.

"Camp Granada." Miché, Mary. Nature Nuts.

"Can You Sound Just like Me?" Grammer, Red. Can You Sound Just like Me?

"Candy Man." Monet, Lisa. My Best Friend.

"Candy Man, Salty Dog." Sharon, Lois and Bram. Great Big Hits.

"Candy Man, Salty Dog." Sharon, Lois and Bram. One Elephant, Deux Elephants.

"Candy Man, Salty Dog." Sharon, Lois and Bram. One, Two, Three, Four, Live!

"Charlie over the Ocean." Sharon, Lois and Bram. Singing 'n Swinging.

"Che Che Koolay." Sharon, Lois and Bram. Smorgasbord.

"Crocodiles Eat Pizza with Their Tails." Peanutbutterjam. Incredibly Spreadable.

"Did You Feed My Cow?" Jenkins, Ella. You'll Sing a Song and I'll Sing a Song.

"Did You Feed My Cow?" Sharon, Lois and Bram. Smorgasbord.

"Discover and Identify." Penner, Fred. What a Day!

"Down by the Bay." Wee Sing Silly Songs.

"Even If You Had." Wellington, Bill. WOOF Hits the Road.

"Even If You Had." Wellington, Bill. WOOF's Greatest Bits.

"Everybody Ought to Know." Sweet Honey in the Rock. All for Freedom.

"Flea, Fly, Mosquito." Sharon, Lois and Bram. One Elephant, Deux Elephants.

"Fun-a-Rooey." Kinnoin, Dave. Fun-a-Rooey.

"Going on a Lion Hunt." Parachute Express. Circle of Friends.

"Going on a Picnic." Raffi. Corner Grocery Store.

"Good Morning Sunshine." Grunsky, Jack. Waves of Wonder.

"The Green Grass Grows All Around." Wee Sing Silly Songs.

"Grizzly Bear." Wee Sing Fun 'n' Folk.

"Hand Jive." Greg and Steve. We All Live Together, Vol. 4.

"Healthy Planet, Healthy People." The Van Manens. Healthy Planet, Healthy People.

"Hi-Dee-Ho." Sharon, Lois and Bram. The Elephant Show Record.

"Hiding in My Pocket." Peanutbutterjam. Simply Singable.

"I Am a Pizza." Alsop, Peter. Wha'd'ya Wanna Do?

"I Am a Pizza." Arnold, Linda. Peppermint Wings.

"I Am a Pizza." Diamond, Charlotte. 10 Carrot Diamond.

"I Like Potatoes." Greg and Steve. We All Live Together, Vol. 5.

"I Like Science and Nature." Janet and Judy. Musical Almanac.

"I'm a Dirty Kid." Buchman, Rachel. Hello Rachel! Hello Children!

"Juba." Nagler, Eric. Improvise with Eric Nagler.

"La-La Man." Parachute Express. Circle of Friends.

"Let's Go to the Market." Greg and Steve. We All Live Together, Vol. 5.

"Life Is." Rosenshontz. Rosenshontz Tickles You.

"Little Sir Echo." Greg and Steve. We All Live Together, Vol. 1.

"Little Sir Echo." Sharon, Lois and Bram. Great Big Hits.

"Little Sir Echo." Sharon, Lois and Bram. Sing A to Z.

"Lonesome Valley." Seeger, Pete. Family Concert.

"Many Cows." Pease, Tom. Boogie Boogie Boogie.

"May-Ree-Mack." Jenkins, Ella. You'll Sing a Song and I'll Sing a Song.

"Miss Mary Mack." Jenkins, Ella. You'll Sing a Song and I'll Sing a Song.

"Miss McFanny." Peanutbutterjam. Simply Singable.

"My Aunt Came Back." Nagler, Eric. Fiddle Up a Tune.

"My Dog Treed Rabbit." Nagler, Eric. Fiddle Up a Tune.

"My Mama's Calling Me." Shake It to the One That You Love the Best.

"My Name Is Joe." Wellington, Bill. WOOF Hits Home.

"My Name Is Joe." Wellington, Bill. WOOF's Greatest Bits.

"The Number Game." Greg and Steve. We All Live Together, Vol. 5.

"The Number Rock." Greg and Steve. We All Live Together, Vol. 2.

"Oh, John the Rabbit." Seeger, Mike and Peggy. American Songs for Children.

"Oh, You Can't Get to Heaven." Wee Sing Silly Songs.

"Ol' John the Rabbit." Sharon, Lois and Bram. Mainly Mother Goose.

"Ol' Texas." Cassidy, Nancy. Kids' Songs 2.

"Old Texas." Sharon, Lois and Bram. One, Two, Three, Four, Live!

"The One and Only Me." Atkinson, Lisa. The One and Only Me.

"One World." (Lois LaFond) Early Ears: Songs Just for 6 Year Olds.

"One World." LaFond, Lois. One World.

"Packin' for My Hike." Miché, Mary. Nature Nuts.

"Part of the Family." (Lois LaFond) Early Ears: Songs Just for 6 Year Olds.

"Part of the Family." LaFond, Lois. One World.

"Peanut Butter and Jelly." Fink, Cathy. Grandma Slid down the Mountain.

"People Are Animals, Too!" Quackity Yakity Bop.

"Pinyebo." Sharon, Lois and Bram. Singing 'n Swinging.

"Polly the Parrot." Grunsky, Jack. Waves of Wonder.

"Promises to Keep." Sharon, Lois and Bram. One, Two, Three, Four, Live!

"Pufferbellies." Sharon, Lois and Bram. All the Fun You Can Sing!

"Pufferbellies." Sharon, Lois and Bram. Great Big Hits.

"Pufferbellies." Sharon, Lois and Bram. In the Schoolyard.

"Pufferbellies." Sharon, Lois and Bram. One, Two, Three, Four, Live!

"Ragg Mopp." Penner, Fred. Happy Feet.

"Sabunana Kusasa." Pease, Tom. Boogie Boogie Boogie.

"Say Hello." Greg and Steve. Kidding Around.

"Scat like That." Greg and Steve. On the Move.

"Two Hands Four Hands." Grammer, Red. Down the Do-Re-Mi.

"Wascawy Wabbit." (Lois LaFond) Early Ears: Songs Just for 5 Year Olds.

"Wascawy Wabbit." LaFond, Lois. One World.

"We Are Flowers." The Van Manens. We Recycle.

"When Cows Get Up in the Morning." Carfra, Pat. Babes, Beasts, and Birds.

"Where Is Thumbkin?" Sharon, Lois and Bram. In the Schoolyard.

"Yes, I Can!" Peanutbutterjam. Simply Singable.

"Les Zombies et les Loups-Garous." Raffi. Corner Grocery Store.

Cumulative Songs

Cumulative songs add verse upon verse and then usually repeat them in reverse order. A good example is the traditional "I Had a Rooster." A pattern is established. "I had a rooster, the rooster pleased me. I fed my rooster 'neath the old greenwood tree, My little rooster went cock-a-doodle-doo-dee-doodle-dee-doodle-dee-doodle-dee-do." You can repeat this pattern adding a cat, a dog, a cow, and so on, listing all of the previous animals during the chorus.

> *My little cow went "moo,"*
> *My little dog went "woof,"*
> *My little cat went "meow,"*
> *My little rooster went "cock-a-doodle-do-*
> *dee-doodle-dee-doodle-dee-doodle-dee-do."*

Here are more great cumulative songs:

"Big Old Cat." Lewis, Shari. Lamb Chop's Sing-Along, Play-Along.

"The Big Picture." The Chenille Sisters. The Big Picture.

"Birthday Cake." Parachute Express. Sunny Side Up.

"Bought Me a Cat." Seeger, Pete. American Folk Songs for Children.

"Bought Me a Cat." Wee Sing Fun 'n' Folk.

"The Choo Choo Song." (Karan and the Musical Medicine Show) Early Ears: Songs Just for 1 Year Olds.

"Down by the Sea." Grammer, Red. Down the Do-Re-Mi.

"Dry Bones." Wee Sing Silly Songs.

"E Compare." Penner, Fred. Fred Penner's Place.

"Everybody Happy." Sharon, Lois and Bram. All the Fun You Can Sing!

"Everybody Happy." Sharon, Lois and Bram. The Elephant Show Record.

"Fiddle Eye Fee." Neat, Roxanne, and David Stoeri. Dance, Boatman, Dance.

"Fi-Fiddle-Diddle-I-Ay." Parachute Express. Over Easy.

"Green Grass Grew All Around." Seeger, Pete. Songs and Stories for Little Children.

"Green Grass Grew All Around." Wee Sing Silly Songs.

"Green Grass Grows All Around." Roth, Kevin. Oscar, Bingo, and Buddies.

"Green Grass Grows All Around." Roth, Kevin. Travel Song Sing Alongs.

"Green Grass Grows All Around." Seeger, Pete. Abiyoyo and Other Story Songs for Children.

"Greenwood Tree." Quackity Yakity Bop.

"Had a Little Rooster." Wee Sing Fun 'n' Folk.

"I Had a Rooster." Weissman, Jackie. Peanut Butter, Tarzan, and Roosters.

"I Have a Song to Sing, O!" Peter, Paul and Mary. Peter, Paul and Mommy.

"I Know an Old Lady." Ives, Burl. The Best of Burl's for Boys and Girls.

"I Know an Old Lady." Seeger, Pete. Stories and Songs for Little Children.

"I Know an Old Lady Who Swallowed a Fly." Peter, Paul and Mary. Peter, Paul and Mommy, Too.

"I Know an Old Lady Who Swallowed a Fly." Roth, Kevin. Unbearable Bears.

"In My Pocket." Charette, Rick. Chickens on Vacation.

"Jelly, Jelly in My Belly." Sharon, Lois and Bram. The Elephant Show Record.

"Keep On Dancing." Avni, Fran. Artichokes and Brussel Sprouts.

"My Hand on My Head." Wee Sing Silly Songs.

"Nobody Else like Me." Walker, Mary Lu. The Frog's Party.

"Old King Cole." Wellington, Bill. WOOF Hits the Road.

"Old King Cole." Wellington, Bill. WOOF's Greatest Bits.

"Old MacDonald Had a Band." Raffi. Singable Songs for the Very Young.

"Old MacDonald Had a Farm." Wee Sing.

"The Old MacDonald Swing." Janet and Judy. Hotbilly Hits.

"Once an Austrian Went Yodeling." Wee Sing Silly Songs.

"Parade Came Marching." Chapin, Tom. Family Tree.

"The Planting Song." Buckner, Janice. Little Friends for Little Folks.

"Plenty of Room." Chapin, Tom. Family Tree.

"Rainbow 'round Me." Pelham, Ruth. Under One Sky.

"Rattlin' Bog." Grammer, Red. Down the Do-Re-Mi.

"The Rattlin' Bog." Penner, Fred. Poco.

"Rattlin' Bog." Sharon, Lois and Bram. In the Schoolyard.

"The Rattlin' Bog." Wee Sing Fun 'n' Folk.

"Rig-a-Jig-Jig." Sharon, Lois and Bram. The Elephant Show Record.

"Rock 'n' Roll Rhythm Band." Greg and Steve. We All Live Together, Vol. 5.

"Sailing to the Sea." Chapin, Tom. Mother Earth.

"Shakin' It." Parachute Express. Shakin' It!

"Share It." Rosenshontz. Share It.

"Something in My Shoe." Raffi. Rise and Shine.

"A Song of One." Chapin, Tom. Mother Earth.

"Staple in My Sock." Charette, Rick. Alligator in the Elevator.

"State Laughs." Chapin, Tom. Moonboat.

"There Was an Old Lady." Penner, Fred. Ebeneezer Sneezer.

"There's a Hole in the Bottom of the Sea." Wee Sing Silly Songs.

"There's a Hole in the Middle of the Sea." Grammer, Red. Red Grammer's Favorite Sing Along Songs.

"The Train Song." Buckner, Janice. All Aboard the Learn Along Train.

"The Train Song." Buckner, Janice. Little Friends for Little Folks.

"What Will I Take to the Moon?" Parachute Express. Happy to Be Here.

"When I Build My House." Parachute Express. Circle of Friends.

"When I First Came to This Land." Harley, Bill. 50 Ways to Fool Your Mother.

"When I First Came to This Land." Rosenthal, Phil. The Paw Paw Patch.

"When I Was a Baby." Carfra, Pat. Songs for Sleepyheads and Out-of-Beds.

"Wiggle in My Toe." Scruggs, Joe. Late Last Night.

"World of Make-Believe." Parachute Express. Feel the Music.

Rounds

"Alvin the Alligator." Rockow, Corrine. I Sing Every Day of My Life.

"Are You Sleeping (Frère Jacques)." Wee Sing Sing-Alongs.

"Bedtime Round." Chapin, Tom. Billy the Squid.

"Black Socks." Harley, Bill. Monsters in the Bathroom.

"Boom Boom." Bishop, Heather. Bellybutton.

"Catches." Chapin, Tom. Moonboat.

"Chairs to Mend." Wee Sing Sing-Alongs.

"Come Follow." Sharon, Lois and Bram. Stay Tuned.

"Come Follow." Wee Sing Sing-Alongs.

"Dona Nobis." Wee Sing Sing-Alongs.

"Down by the Station." Dallas, Patti, and Laura Baron. Playtime Parade.

"Duchess for Tea." Neat, Roxanne, and David Stoeri. Dance, Boatman, Dance.

"Fish and Chips and Vinegar." Sharon, Lois and Bram. All the Fun You Can Sing!

"Fish and Chips and Vinegar." Sharon, Lois and Bram. Great Big Hits.

"Fish and Chips and Vinegar." Sharon, Lois and Bram. Happy Birthday.

"For Health and Strength." Wee Sing Sing-Alongs.

"Four Seasons." Baron, Laura, and Patti Dallas. Songs for the Earth.

"Frère Jacques." Wee Sing around the World.

"The Frog in the Bog." Wee Sing Fun 'n' Folk.

"Frog Round." Wee Sing Sing-Alongs.

"The Ghost of John." Sharon, Lois and Bram. Stay Tuned.

"Grasshoppers Three." Quackity Yakity Bop.

"Grasshoppers Three." Wee Sing Fun 'n' Folk.

"Grow in Your Own Sweet Way." Chapin, Tom. Moonboat.

"Growing Song." Atkinson, Lisa. I Wanna Tickle the Fish.

"Hark to the Street Cries." Rockow, Corrine. I Sing Every Day of My Life.

"Hey, Ho! Nobody Home." Wee Sing Sing-Alongs.

"I Walk in Beauty." Rogers, Sally. Piggyback Planet.

"Jamais On N'a Vu." Sharon, Lois and Bram. Singing 'n Swinging.

"Junk Round." Rogers, Sally. Piggyback Planet.

"Kookaburra." Dallas, Patti, and Laura Baron. Playtime Parade.

"Kookaburra." Miché, Mary. Earthy Tunes.

"Kookaburra." Staines, Bill. The Happy Wanderer.

"Kookaburra." Wee Sing Sing-Alongs.

"Let Us Sing Together." Wee Sing Sing-Alongs.

"Little Tom Tinker." Wee Sing Sing-Alongs.

"Little Tommy Tinker." Sharon, Lois and Bram. One, Two, Three, Four, Live!

"Little Tommy Tinker." Sharon, Lois and Bram. One Elephant, Deux Elephants.

"Make New Friends." Sweet Honey in the Rock. All for Freedom.

"Make New Friends." Wee Sing Sing-Alongs.

"Matthew, Mark, Luke and John." Sharon, Lois and Bram. In the Schoolyard.

"Music Alone Shall Live." Wee Sing Sing-Alongs.

"Now All the Woods Are Waking." Monet, Lisa. My Best Friend.

"Oh, How Lovely." Gemini. Good Mischief.

"Oh, How Lovely." Wee Sing Sing-Alongs.

"One Earth." Arnold, Linda. Happiness Cake.

"Peace Is the World Smiling." Peace Is the World Smiling.

"Peace Round." Pease, Tom. Boogie Boogie Boogie.

"Pretty Planet." Chapin, Tom. Family Tree.

"Promises to Keep." Sharon, Lois and Bram. One, Two, Three, Four, Live!

"Pufferbellies." Sharon, Lois and Bram. All the Fun You Can Sing!

"Pufferbellies." Sharon, Lois and Bram. Great Big Hits.

"Pufferbellies." Sharon, Lois and Bram. In the Schoolyard.

"Pufferbellies." Sharon, Lois and Bram. One, Two, Three, Four, Live!

"The Rain Round." Rogers, Sally. Piggyback Planet.

"Rainwater." Scooter. Calling All Kids.

"A Ram Sam Sam." The Flyers. Family Hug.

"A Ram Sam Sam." Wee Sing Sing-Alongs.

"Reuben and Rachel." Wee Sing Sing-Alongs.

"Ride a Cock Horse." Dallas, Patti, and Laura Baron. Playtime Parade.

"Rounds." Chapin, Tom. Family Tree.

"Row, Row, Row." Raffi. Rise and Shine.

"Row, Row, Row, Your Boat." Bartels, Joanie. Bathtime Magic.

"Row, Row, Row, Your Boat." Wee Sing Sing-Alongs.

"Scotland's Burning." Wee Sing Sing-Alongs.

"Seasons." Avni, Fran. Daisies and Ducklings.

"Sing Together." Wee Sing Sing-Alongs.

"Sweetly Sings the Donkey." Wee Sing Sing-Alongs.

"Three Blind Mice." Quackity Yakity Bop.

"Three Blind Mice." Sharon, Lois and Bram. Mainly Mother Goose.

"Three Blind Mice." Wee Sing Sing-Alongs.

"White Coral Bells." Wee Sing Sing-Alongs.

"Why Shouldn't My Goose." Wee Sing Sing-Alongs.

Songs in Foreign Languages

African Languages

"African Numbers." Sweet Honey in the Rock. I Got Shoes. (Swahili)

"Akwa Nwa Nere Nnwa." Wee Sing around the World. (Ibo)

"Bebe Moke." Wee Sing around the World. (Lingala)

"Denko." (Sweet Honey in the Rock) Rainbow Sign. (Bambara)

"Ise Oluwa." (Sweet Honey in the Rock) Family Folk Festival. (Yoruba)

"Ise Oluwa." Sweet Honey in the Rock. All for Freedom. (Yoruba)

"Kanyoni Kanja." Wee Sing around the World. (Kikuyu)

"Lala Gahle." Tracey, Paul. The Rainbow Kingdom. (Zulu)

"Sabunana Kusasa." Pease, Tom. Boogie Boogie Boogie. (Zulu)

"She She Ko Le." Pirtle, Sarah. The Wind Is Telling Secrets. (from Nigeria)

"Siyanibingelela." Grunsky, Jack. Waves of Wonder. (Zulu)

"Somagwaza." Sweet Honey in the Rock. I Got Shoes. (Bantu)

"Somagwaza/Hey, Motswala." Peter, Paul and Mary. Peter, Paul and Mommy, Too. (Bantu)

"Tama Tama Tamali." Sweet Honey in the Rock. I Got Shoes. (from Guinea, West Africa)

"Thula Baba." Grunsky, Jack. Waves of Wonder. (Xhosa)

"Tue Tue." Wee Sing around the World. (from Ghana)

Cantonese

"May There Always Be Sunshine." Diamond, Charlotte. 10 Carrot Diamond.

Chasidic

"Chirri Bim." Sharon, Lois and Bram. Smorgasbord.

Danish

"En Enebaer Busk." Wee Sing around the World.

Finnish

"Piiri Pieni Pyörii." Wee Sing around the World.

French

"A La Queue." Carfra, Pat. Babes, Beasts, and Birds.

"African Numbers." Sweet Honey in the Rock. I Got Shoes.

"Ah Si Mon Moine." Sharon, Lois and Bram. In the Schoolyard.

"Au Galop." Carfra, Pat. Songs for Sleepyheads and Out-of-Beds.

"La Bastringue." Diamond, Charlotte. Diamond in the Rough.

"La Bastringue." Sharon, Lois and Bram. One, Two, Three, Four, Live!

"Bats Ta Pate." Diamond, Charlotte. My Bear Gruff.

"Berceuse." Carfra, Pat. Songs for Sleepyheads and Out-of-Beds.

"Bon Soir, Mes Amis." Penner, Fred. Ebeneezer Sneezer.

"Collinda." Diamond, Charlotte. Diamond in the Rough.

"Dans Tout le Monde Entier." Mish, Michael. A Kid's Eye View of the Environment.

"The Days of the Week." Diamond, Charlotte. Diamond in the Rough.

"Donne-Moi la Main." Diamond, Charlotte. Diamond in the Rough.

"En Roulent Ma Boule." Penner, Fred. Ebeneezer Sneezer.

"Fais Do Do." Sharon, Lois and Bram. Mainly Mother Goose.

"Fais Do Do, Colas." Shake It to the One That You Love the Best.

"Fais Dodo." Carfra, Pat. Songs for Sleepyheads and Out-of-Beds.

"Fais Dodo." Raffi. One Light, One Sun.

"First Lullaby." Herdman, Priscilla. Stardreamer.

"First Lullaby." Staines, Bill. The Happy Wanderer.

"Frère Jacques." Raffi. Corner Grocery Store.

"Frère Jacques." Wee Sing around the World.

"Ho Ho Watanay." Carfra, Pat. Lullabies and Laughter with the Lullaby Lady.

"I Am a Pizza." Diamond, Charlotte. 10 Carrot Diamond.

"J'ai Perdu le 'Do' De Ma Clarinette." Diamond, Charlotte. 10 Carrot Diamond.

"Jamais On N'a Vu." Sharon, Lois and Bram. Singing 'n Swinging.

"May There Always Be Sunshine." Diamond, Charlotte. 10 Carrot Diamond.

"Michaud." Raffi. Rise and Shine.

"Michaud." Sharon, Lois and Bram. One Elephant, Deux Elephants.

"Monte Sur Un Elephant." Sharon, Lois and Bram. Singing 'n Swinging.

"One Elephant, Deux Elephants." Sharon, Lois and Bram. One Elephant, Deux Elephants.

"Petit Papa." Sharon, Lois and Bram. Happy Birthday.

"Les Petites Marionettes." Raffi. More Singable Songs.

"Les Petites Poissons." Sharon, Lois and Bram. Sing A to Z.

"La Poulette Grise." Carfra, Pat. Babes, Beasts, and Birds.

"P'tit Galop Pour Mamou." (Michael Doucet) Rainbow Sign.

"Rainbows." LaFond, Lois. I Am Who I Am!

"Savez-Vous Planter Des Choux." Raffi. Everything Grows.

"Savez-Vous Planter Des Choux." Sharon, Lois and Bram. Mainly Mother Goose.

"Shanty Medley." Sharon, Lois and Bram. One, Two, Three, Four, Live!

"Sur Le Pont." Sharon, Lois and Bram. Smorgasbord.

"Sur Le Pont D'Avignon." Raffi. Corner Grocery Store.

"Teagan's Lullaby." Penner, Fred. The Cat Came Back.

"Tête, Epaules." Raffi. Rise and Shine.

"To Everyone in All the World." Raffi. Baby Beluga.

"We're Gonna Shine." Penner, Fred. Fred Penner's Place.

"Y'a Un Chat." Diamond, Charlotte. My Bear Gruff.

"Y'a Un Rat." Raffi. Corner Grocery Store.

"Les Zombies et les Loups-Garous." Raffi. Corner Grocery Store.

German

"Alle Meine Entlein." Wee Sing around the World.

"May There Always Be Sunshine." Diamond, Charlotte. 10 Carrot Diamond.

Greek

"Charoumena Genethlia." Sharon, Lois and Bram. Happy Birthday.

"Pou'n-do To Dachtilidi." Wee Sing around the World.

Hawaiian

"Haleakala." Crow, Dan. A Friend, A Laugh, A Walk in the Woods.

"Nani Wale Na Hala." Wee Sing around the World.

Hebrew

"Tzena Tzena." Sharon, Lois and Bram. All the Fun You Can Sing!

"Tzena Tzena." Sharon, Lois and Bram. Sing A to Z.

"Zum Gali Gali." Wee Sing around the World.

Iroquois

"Ho Ho Watanay." Carfra, Pat. Lullabies and Laughter with the Lullaby Lady.

"Ho Ho Watanay." Sharon, Lois and Bram. One Elephant, Deux Elephants.

Italian

"Mio Galletto." Wee Sing around the World.

Japanese

"African Numbers." Sweet Honey in the Rock. I Got Shoes.

"Ame, Ame." Wee Sing around the World.

"Chatto Matte, Kudasi." Jenkins, Ella. I Know the Colors of the Rainbow.

"Haru Ga Kitu." Raffi. Everything Grows.

"Haru Ga Kitu." Raffi. Raffi on Broadway.

"One Crane." Pease, Tom. Wobbi-Do-Wop.

Korean

"Arirang." Wee Sing around the World.

Mandarin

"Fong Swei." Wee Sing around the World.

Maori

"Epo I Tai Tai E." Wee Sing around the World.

Navajo

"Rain Song." (Sharon Burch) Rainbow Sign.

Norwegian

"Ro, Ro Til Fiskeskjær." Wee Sing around the World.

Omaha

"Uhe' Basho Sho." Wee Sing around the World.

Persian

"Attal, Mattal." Wee Sing around the World.

Polish

"Sto Lat." Sharon, Lois and Bram. Happy Birthday.

Portuguese

"Ciranda." Wee Sing around the World.
"Samba de General." Quackity Yakity Bop.

Russian

"May There Always Be Sunshine." Diamond, Charlotte. 10
    Carrot Diamond.
"May There Always Be Sunshine." Pease, Tom. Boogie Boogie
    Boogie.
"May There Always Be Sunshine." Pirtle, Sarah. Two Hands
    Hold the Earth.
"May There Always Be Sunshine." Raffi. Raffi on Broadway.
"One World." Monet, Lisa. Jump Down.
"Vesyoliye Gusi." Wee Sing around the World.

Sioux

"Sioux Indian Lullaby Chant." (Lois LaFond) Early Ears: Songs
    Just for 1 Year Olds.

Spanish

"African Numbers." Sweet Honey in the Rock. I Got Shoes.

"La bamba." Cassidy, Nancy. Kids' Songs 2.

"La bamba." Diamond, Charlotte. 10 Carrot Diamond.

"La bamba." Grammer, Red. Red Grammer's Favorite Sing Along Songs.

"La bamba." Monet, Lisa. My Best Friend.

"La bamba." Sharon, Lois and Bram. In the Schoolyard.

"Brush Your Teeth (Cepíllense los dientes)." (Fred Miller) Early Ears: Songs Just for 5 Year Olds.

"Caballito blanco." Sharon, Lois and Bram. Sing A to Z.

"Colors/colores." (Lois LaFond) Early Ears: Songs Just for 5 Year Olds.

"Colors/colores." LaFond, Lois. I Am Who I Am!

"El coquí." Wee Sing around the World.

"The Days of the Week." Diamond, Charlotte. Diamond in the Rough.

"De colores." Pirtle, Sarah. Two Hands Hold the Earth.

"De colores." Raffi. One Light, One Sun.

"De colores." Raffi. Raffi on Broadway.

"De colores." Tickle Tune Typhoon. Hearts and Hands.

"El gallo pinto." (Claudia Gomez) Family Folk Festival.

"Guantanamera." Seeger, Peter. Family Concert.

"Las mañanitas." Sharon, Lois and Bram. Happy Birthday.

"May There Always Be Sunshine." Diamond, Charlotte. 10 Carrot Diamond.

"Mi burro." Wee Sing around the World.

"Mi chacra." Wee Sing around the World.

"Mi cuerpo hace música." Pirtle, Sarah. The Wind Is Telling Secrets.

"Months of the Year." Greg and Steve. We All Live Together, Vol. 2.

"Nanita Nana." Grunsky, Jack. Waves of Wonder.

"One World." Monet, Lisa. Jump Down.

"Paz y libertad." (Jose-Luis Orozco) Rainbow Sign.

"Pin Pón." Wee Sing around the World.

"Los pollitos." Wee Sing around the World.

"El sereno." Sharon, Lois and Bram. Mainly Mother Goose.

"Somos el barco." Cassidy, Nancy. Kids' Songs Sleepyheads.

"Somos el barco." (John McCutcheon) Rainbow Sign.

"Somos el barco." McCutcheon, John. Mail Myself to You.

"Somos el barco." Pease, Tom. I'm Gonna Reach.

"Somos el barco." Peter, Paul and Mary. Peter, Paul and Mommy, Too.

"Somos el barco." The Singing Rainbow Youth Ensemble. Head First and Belly Down.

"Somos el barco/We Are the Boat." Harley, Bill. 50 Ways to Fool Your Mother.

"Tell Me How to Say . . .?" Marin, Cheech. My Name Is Cheech, the School Bus Driver.

"We Are the Boat." Seeger, Pete. Family Concert.

"Welcome to My Farm." Phipps, Bonnie. Monsters' Holiday.

"We're Gonna Shine." Penner, Fred. Fred Penner's Place.

Swedish

"Sma Grodorna." Wee Sing around the World.

Tamil (from India)

"Anilae, Anilae." Wee Sing around the World.

Yiddish

"Der Rebbe Elimelech." Sharon, Lois and Bram. Mainly Mother Goose.

"Tsu Dayn Gerburtstog." Sharon, Lois and Bram. Happy Birthday.

"Tumbalalaika, Play Balalaika." Jenkins, Ella. I Know the Colors of the Rainbow.

Songs That Feature Sound Effects

The following tunes employ a variety of sounds that the children can make during the course of the song. Many of the fun songs listed below allow the kids to make animal, musical instrument, vehicle, or nonsensical noises.

"Band of Sounds." Schneider, Bob. When You Dream a Dream.

"The Bear That Snores." Roth, Kevin. Unbearable Bears.

"The Bibble Song." (June Rachelson-Ospa) Early Ears: Songs Just for 2 Year Olds.

"Big Brass Band." Grammer, Red. Can You Sound Just like Me?

"Bought Me a Cat." Seeger, Mike and Peggy. American Folk Songs for Children.

"Bought Me a Cat." Wee Sing Fun 'n' Folk.

"The Bus Song." Cassidy, Nancy. Kids' Songs 2.

"Busy Box Band." Scruggs, Joe. Bahamas Pajamas.

"Can You Sound Just like Me?" Grammer, Red. Can You Sound Just like Me?

"A Chicken Ain't Nothin' but a Bird." Phipps, Bonnie. Monsters' Holiday.

"The Choo Choo Song." (Karan and the Musical Medicine Show) Early Ears: Songs Just for 1 Year Olds.

"The Circus Song." (Maria Muldaur) Family Folk Festival.

"The Circus Song." Muldaur, Maria. On the Sunny Side.

"Country Store." Noah, Tim. Kaddywompas.

"The Crazy Traffic Light." Rappin' Rob. The Rappin' Rob Rap.

"Dave the Friendly Ghost." The Van Manens. We Recycle.

"Doggie." Grammer, Red. Can You Sound Just like Me?

"Down by the Sea." Grammer, Red. Down the Do-Re-Mi.

"Down on Grandpa's Farm." Raffi. One Light, One Sun.

"Down on the Farm." Greg and Steve. We All Live Together, Vol. 5.

"Down on the Farm." Parachute Express. Circle of Friends.

"Ducks Like Rain." Raffi. Rise and Shine.

"Five Speckled Frogs." Quackity Yakity Bop.

"The Foolish Frog." Diamond, Charlotte. Diamond in the Rough.

"Foolish Frog." Seeger, Pete. Stories and Songs for Little Children.

"The Fox." Peter, Paul and Mary. Peter, Paul and Mommy, Too.

"Gettin' Up Time." Palmer, Hap. Peek-a-Boo.

"Go'n to Gramma's Farm." Wozniak, Doug. Hugs and Kisses.

"Grandpa's Farm." Fink, Cathy, and Marcy Marxer. A Cathy and Marcy Collection for Kids.

"Grandpa's Farm." Marxer, Marcy. Jump Children.

"Grandpa's Farm." Sharon, Lois and Bram. Great Big Hits.

"Grandpa's Farm." Sharon, Lois and Bram. Sing A to Z.

"Greenwood Tree." Quackity Yakity Bop.

"Had a Little Rooster." Wee Sing Fun 'n' Folk.

"Halloween Song." Phipps, Bonnie. Monsters' Holiday.

"Heading On Down to the Barn." Grammer, Red. Down the Do-Re-Mi.

"Hey, Ev'rybody." Alsop, Peter. Take Me with You.

"Hey, Mabel!" Buckner, Janice. All Aboard the Learn Along Train.

"Howling at the Moon." Gemini. Two of a Kind.

"I Can Do Something I Bet You Can't Do." Peanutbutterjam. Incredibly Spreadable.

"I Had a Rooster." (Pete Seeger) Family Folk Festival.

"I Had a Rooster." Penner, Fred. The Cat Came Back.

"I Know an Old Lady Who Swallowed a Fly." Peter, Paul and Mary. Peter, Paul and Mommy, Too.

"I See a Horsie." Weissman, Jackie. Peanut Butter, Tarzan, and Roosters.

"I Wanna Be a Dog." Alsop, Peter. Wha'd'ya Wanna Do?

"I Wanna Be a Dog." Diamond, Charlotte. 10 Carrot Diamond.

"I'm So Mad I Could Scream." Weissman, Jackie. Peanut Butter, Tarzan, and Roosters.

"In My Pocket." Charette, Rick. Chickens on Vacation.

"A Jolly Old Pig." Carfra, Pat. Songs for Sleepyheads and Out-of-Beds.

"Jungle Walk." Buckner, Janice. All Aboard the Learn Along Train.

"Late at Night When I'm Hungry." Charette, Rick. Bubble Gum and Other Songs for Hungry Kids.

"Let's Make Some Noise." Raffi. Everything Grows.

"Listen to the Water." Schneider, Bob. Listen to the Children.

"The Little Pig." Seeger, Mike and Peggy. American Folk Songs for Children.

"The Little White Duck." Bartels, Joanie. Bathtime Magic.

"The Little White Duck." Kaye, Danny. Danny Kaye for Children.

"Lunchtime Lion." Gibson, Dee, and Joe Scruggs. Songs to Brighten Your Day.

"Marvellous Toy." Atkinson, Lisa. I Wanna Tickle the Fish.

"The Marvellous Toy." Carfra, Pat. Lullabies and Laughter with the Lullaby Lady.

"The Marvellous Toy." Gemini. Good Mischief.

"The Marvellous Toy." Paxton, Tom. The Marvellous Toy.

"The Marvellous Toy." Penner, Fred. Ebeneezer Sneezer.

"The Marvelous Toy." Drake, David HB. Kid-Stuff.

"Marvelous Toy." Penner, Fred. Collections.

"The Marvelous Toy." Peter, Paul and Mary. Peter, Paul and Mommy.

"Monster Walk." Schneider, Bob. When You Dream a Dream.

"The New Wheels on the Bus." Rappin' Rob. The Rappin' Rob Rap.

"Noise." Rory. Make-Believe Day.

"Old MacDonald." Little Richard. Shake It All About.

"Old MacDonald Had a Band." Raffi. Singable Songs for the Very Young.

"Old MacDonald Had a Farm." Roth, Kevin. Oscar, Bingo, and Buddies.

"Old MacDonald Had a Farm." Wee Sing.

"Old MacDonald Had a 'Whzz.'" Weissman, Jackie. Peanut Butter, Tarzan, and Roosters.

"The Old Sow." Sharon, Lois and Bram. One Elephant, Deux Elephants.

"The Old Sow Song." Penner, Fred. Ebeneezer Sneezer.

"On the Funny Farm." Rosenshontz. Uh-Oh.

"Once an Austrian Went Yodeling." Wee Sing Silly Songs.

"One Day My Best Friend Barbara Turned into a Frog." Polisar, Barry Louis. Old Dog, New Tricks.

"Parade Came Marching." Chapin, Tom. Family Tree.

"Preacher Herman." Chapin, Tom. Billy the Squid.

"Princess Di's Distress." Chapin, Tom. Moonboat.

"Pufferbellies." Sharon, Lois and Bram. All the Fun You Can Sing!

"Pufferbellies." Sharon, Lois and Bram. Great Big Hits.

"Pufferbellies." Sharon, Lois and Bram. In the Schoolyard.

"Pufferbellies." Sharon, Lois and Bram. One, Two, Three, Four, Live!

"Quit That Snorin'." Roth, Kevin. The Sandman.

"Sailing to the Sea." Chapin, Tom. Mother Earth.

"She'll Be Comin' round the Mountain." Sharon, Lois and Bram. One Elephant, Deux Elephants.

"She'll Be Comin' round the Mountain." Wee Sing Sing-Alongs.

"She'll Be Comin' round the Mountain." Cassidy, Nancy. Kids' Songs 2.

"She'll Be Comin' round the Mountain." Greg and Steve. We All Live Together, Vol. 2.

"She'll Be Comin' round the Mountain." Seeger, Pete. Stories and Songs for Little Children.

"She'll Be Comin' round the Mountain." Sharon, Lois and Bram. Great Big Hits.

"Sing a Whale Song." Chapin, Tom. Moonboat.

"So Much to Hear." Palmer, Hap. More Baby Songs.

"Something in My Shoe." Raffi. Rise and Shine.

"Sounds from A to Z." Rosenshontz. Share It.

"Staple in My Sock." Charette, Rick. Alligator in the Elevator.

"Stop and Listen." Diamond, Charlotte. Diamonds and Dragons.

"This Little Song." Lewis, Shari. Lamb Chop's Sing-Along, Play-Along.

"The Train Song." Buckner, Janice. All Aboard the Learn Along Train.

"The Train Song." Buckner, Janice. Little Friends for Little Folks.

"Up in the Sky Where the Whales Are." LaFond, Lois. I Am Who I Am!

"Watermelon." McCutcheon, John. Family Garden.

"Welcome to My Farm." Phipps, Bonnie. Monsters' Holiday.

"What Will I Take to the Moon?" Parachute Express. Happy to Be Here.

"Wheels on the Bus." Bartels, Joanie. Travelin' Magic.

"Wheels on the Bus." Raffi. Rise and Shine.

"The Wheels on the Bus." Sharon, Lois and Bram. The Elephant Show Record.

"When Cows Get Up in the Morning." Carfra, Pat. Babes, Beasts, and Birds.

"When I Was a Baby." Carfra, Pat. Songs for Sleepyheads and Out-of-Beds.

"When My Shoes Are Loose." Fink, Cathy, and Marxer, Marcy.
Help Yourself.

"Who Am I?" Parachute Express. Feel the Music.

"Woodland Chorus." Shontz, Bill. Animal Tales.

"World of Make-Believe." Parachute Express. Feel the Music.

♪♪ *Appendix A* ♪♪

A Select List of Children's Musical Videos

Many of the performers listed in this book have appeared in musical videos, another often-overlooked medium full of program ideas. View the videos for techniques and tips on how performers interact with their audiences. The following is a select list of some the best, most recent children's musical videos. They are available from many of the same distributors that carry children's musical audio recordings.

Alsop, Peter. *Costume Party.* Moose School Productions, 1988.

Arnold, Linda. *World of Make Believe.* A & M Video, 1992.

Banana Slug String Band. *Dancing with the Earth.* Music for Little People, n.d.

Bartels, Joanie. *The Extra Special Substitute Teacher.* Discovery Music, 1993.

____. *The Rainy Day Adventure.* Discovery Music, 1993.

Cappelli, Frank. *All Aboard the Train.* A & M Video, 1990.

____. *Slap Me Five.* A & M Video, 1990.

Chapin, Tom. *This Pretty Planet.* Sony Kids' Video, 1992.

Charette, Rick. *An Evening with Rick Charette.* Pine Point Record Company, 1989.

Diamond, Charlotte. *Diamonds and Dragons.* Hug Bug Music, 1989.

Gemini. *Fancy That!* Better Communication, 1990.

Greg and Steve. *Greg and Steve's Musical Adventures.* Youngheart Video, 1991.

_____. *Kids in Motion.* Playhouse Video, 1987.

_____. *Live in Concert!* Youngheart Video, 1991.

Harley, Bill. *Who Made This Mess?* A & M Video, 1992.

Jenkins, Ella. *For the Family.* Smithsonian/Folkways, 1991.

_____. *Live! At the Smithsonian.* Smithsonian/Folkways, 1991.

Lewis, Shari. *Lamb Chop's Play Along: Action Songs.* A & M Video, 1992.

_____. *Lamb Chop's Play Along: Let's Make Music.* A & M Video, 1993.

Nagler, Eric. *Making Music with Eric.* Golden Book Video, 1986.

Palmer, Hap. *Baby Songs.* Hi-Tops Video, 1987.

_____. *Even More Baby Songs.* Hi-Tops Video, 1990.

_____. *More Baby Songs.* Hi-Tops Video, 1987.

Penner, Fred. *The Cat Came Back—Live Concert.* Oak Street Music, 1990.

_____. *What a Day.* Oak Street Music, 1993.

Peter, Paul and Mary. *Peter, Paul and Mommy, Too.* Warner Reprise, 1992.

Polisar, Barry Louis. *I'm a 3-Toed, Triple-Eyed, Double-Jointed Dinosaur.* Rainbow Morning Music, 1987.

_____. *My Brother Threw Up on My Stuffed Toy Bunny.* Rainbow Morning Music, 1987.

Raffi. *Raffi in Concert with the Rise and Shine Band.* A & M Video, 1988.

_____. *Raffi on Broadway.* MCA, 1993.

_____. *A Young Children's Concert.* A & M Video, 1984.

Rory. *The Rory Story.* Sony Kids' Video, 1992.

Rosenshontz. *Feel Better Friends.* Golden Book Video, 1988.

_____. *The Teddy Bears' Picnic.* Light-Video, 1991.

Scruggs, Joe. *Joe Scruggs in Concert.* Educational Graphics Press, 1992.

_____. *Joe's First Video.* Educational Graphics Press, 1989.

Seeger, Pete. *Pete Seeger's Family Concert.* Sony Kids' Video, 1992.

A Select List of Children's Musical Videos

Sharon, Lois and Bram. *Back by Popular Demand—Live.* A & M Video, 1987.

_____. *Sing A to Z.* A & M Video, 1992.

Tickle Tune Typhoon. *Let's Be Friends.* Tickle Tune Typhoon Productions, 1989.

The Van Manens. *We Recycle.* People Records, 1992.

 *Appendix B*

Resources

Puppets

Many of the puppets mentioned in the book are distributed by Folkmanis Puppets and can be found in many book and toy stores. To obtain a catalog, contact:

> Folkmanis/Furry Folk Puppets
> 1219 Park Ave.
> Emeryville, CA 94608
> Tel.: (415) 658-7677
> Fax: (415) 654-7756

Organizations

The Children's Music Network.

> Sarah Pirtle writes that "The Children's Music Network exists to support the creation and dissemination of life-affirming, multi-cultural musical forms by and for young people. Our values include cooperation, diversity, the building of self-esteem, respect and responsibility for our environment, and an understanding of non-violence and social justice. Our membership includes music educators, performers, songwriters, teachers, music listeners of all ages, parents, media people, and those involved in all levels of the teaching, recording, promoting, distributing, and singing of children's music." Anyone interested in the Children's Music Network can write to the Children's Music

Network c/o Sarah Pirtle, 61 Main St., Shelburne Falls, MA 01370, or phone Bob Blue at (413) 256-8784.

Distributors of Children's Recorded Music

The distributors listed below are those that I found to carry most of the recordings mentioned in this work. At the time of this writing, only North Side Music carries all 300-plus recordings listed in this book. Free catalogs are available from all distributors.

Chinaberry Book Service
2780 Via Orange Way, Suite B
Spring Valley, CA 91978
Tel.: (800) 777-5205
Fax: (619) 670-5203

Educational Record Center
3233 Burnt Mill Dr., Suite 100
Wilmington, NC 28403-2655
Tel.: (800) 438-1637
Fax: (910) 343-0311

Enrichment Resources
P.O. Box 427
Pembroke, MA 02359
Tel.: (800) 383-8228
Fax: (617) 294-8228

LTD Audio Visual
19 Brain Rd.
Edison, NJ 08817-2303
Tel.: (800) 788-5871
Fax: (908) 494-0731

Music for Little People
P.O. Box 1460
Redway, CA 95560-1460
Tel.: (800) 727-2233
Fax: (707) 923-3241

North Side Music
1314 Birch St.
Eau Claire, WI 54703
Tel.: (800) 828-9046
Fax: (715) 832-4014

Silo Music
P.O. Box 429
South Main St.
Waterbury, VT 05676-0429
Tel.: (800) 342-0295
Fax: (802) 244-6128

♪♫ *Bibliography* ♫♪

Anderson, Leone Castell. *The Wonderful Shrinking Shirt.* Illustrated by Irene Trivas. Niles, Ill.: Albert Whitman, 1983.

Asbjornsen, Peter C., and J. E. Moe. *The Man Who Kept House.* Illustrated by Svend Otto. New York: Macmillan, 1992.

Aylesworth, Jim. *Two Terrible Frights.* Illustrated by Eileen Christelow. New York: Atheneum, 1987.

Barrett, Judith. *Animals Should Definitely Not Wear Clothing.* Illustrated by Ron Barrett. New York: Atheneum, 1970.

Berenstain, Jan and Stan. *The Berenstain Bears and Too Much Birthday.* New York: Random House, 1986.

Berger, Melvin. *Germs Make Me Sick!* Illustrated by Marylin Hafner. New York: Crowell, 1985.

Brown, Marcia. *Stone Soup.* New York: Scribner, 1947.

Brown, Margaret Wise. *Goodnight Moon.* Illustrated by Clement Hurd. New York: HarperCollins, 1947.

Carle, Eric. *A Very Busy Spider.* New York: Philomel, 1984.

____. *A Very Quiet Cricket.* New York: Philomel, 1990.

Cooney, Nancy Evans. *The Wobbly Tooth.* Illustrated by Marylin Hafner. New York: Putnam, 1978.

Crowe, Robert L. *Clyde Monster.* Illustrated by Kay Chorao. New York: Dutton, 1976.

Duke, Kate. *Seven Froggies Went to School.* New York: Dutton, 1985.

Edelman, Elaine. *I Love My Baby Sister (Most of the Time).* Illustrated by Wendy Watson. New York: Lothrop, Lee and Shepard, 1984.

Ehlert, Lois. *Eating the Alphabet: Fruits and Vegetables from A to Z.* San Diego: Harcourt Brace Jovanovich, 1989.

Fulghum, Robert. *All I Really Need to Know I Learned in Kindergarten.* New York: Ivy Books, 1988.

Fyleman, Rose. *A Fairy Went A-Marketing.* Illustrated by Jamichael Henterly. New York: Dutton, 1986.

Galdone, Paul. *Cat Goes Fiddle-I-Fee.* New York: Clarion, 1985.

____. *Over in the Meadow.* Englewood Cliffs, N.J.: Prentice-Hall, 1986.

Ginsburg, Mirra. *Mushroom in the Rain.* Illustrated by Jose Aruego and Ariane Dewey. New York: Macmillan, 1974.

Hoban, Russell. *Bedtime for Francis.* Illustrated by Garth Willams. New York: Harper, 1960.

Hoff, Syd. *Danny and the Dinosaur.* New York: Harper, 1958.

Hurd, Thacher. *Mama Don't Allow.* New York: Harper and Row, 1984.

Hutchins, Pat. *The Doorbell Rang.* New York: Greenwillow, 1986.

____. *Happy Birthday, Sam.* New York: Greenwillow, 1978.

Ipcar, Dahlov. *Hard Scrabble Harvest.* Garden City, N.Y.: Doubleday, 1976.

Karlin, Nurit. *The Tooth Witch.* New York: Lippincott, 1985.

Kent, Jack. *The Caterpillar and the Polliwog.* Englewood Cliffs, N.J.: Prentice-Hall, 1982.

Kimmel, Eric. *Anansi and the Moss Covered Rock.* Illustrated by Janet Stevens. New York: Holiday House, 1988.

____. *Anansi and the Talking Melon.* Illustrated by Janet Stevens. New York: Holiday House, 1994.

____. *Anansi Goes Fishing.* Illustrated by Janet Stevens. New York: Holiday House, 1992.

King, P. E. *Down on the Funny Farm.* Illustrated by Alastair Graham. New York: Random House, 1986.

Lansky, Bruce. *Kids Pick the Funniest Poems.* Illustrated by Stephen Carpenter. Deephaven, Minn.: Meadowbrook Pr., 1991.

Lee, Dennis. *Alligator Pie.* Illustrated by Frank Newfeld. Boston: Houghton Mifflin, 1975.

Lobel, Arnold. *Frog and Toad Together.* New York: Harper and Row, 1972.

London, Jonathan. *Froggy Gets Dressed.* Illustrated by Frank Remkiewicz. New York: Viking, 1992.

Lorenz, Lee. *A Weekend in the Country.* Englewood Cliffs, N.J.: Prentice-Hall, 1984.

Bibliography

Martin, Bill. *Brown Bear, Brown Bear, What Do You See?* Illustrated by Eric Carle. New York: Holt, 1983.

Martin, Bill, and John Archambault. *Barn Dance.* Illustrated by Ted Rand. New York: Holt, 1986.

Mayer, Mercer. *Just Me and My Dad.* New York: Golden Pr., 1977.

____. *There's an Alligator under My Bed.* New York: Dial, 1987.

Mosel, Arlene. *Tikki Tikki Tembo.* New York: Holt, 1968.

Munsch, Robert. *Mud Puddle.* Toronto: Annick Pr., 1982.

Neitzel, Shirley. *The Jacket I Wear in the Snow.* Illustrated by Nancy Winslow Parker. New York: Greenwillow, 1989.

Newman, Fred. *Mouthsounds.* New York: Workman, 1980.

Pinkwater, Daniel Manus. *I Was a Second Grade Werewolf.* New York: Dutton, 1983.

Prelutsky, Jack. *The New Kid on the Block.* Illustrated by James Stevenson. New York: Greenwillow, 1984.

Purdy, Carol. *Iva Dunnit and the Big Wind.* Illustrated by Steven Kellogg. New York: Dial, 1985.

Raffi. *Down by the Bay.* Illustrated by Nadine Bernice Westcott. New York: Crown, 1987.

____. *Five Little Ducks.* Illustrated by Jose Aruego and Ariane Dewey. New York: Crown, 1989.

____. *Shake My Sillies Out.* Words by Bert and Bonnie Simpson. Illustrated by David Allender. New York: Crown, 1987.

____. *Spider on the Floor.* Words by Bill Russell. Illustrated by True Kelley. New York: Crown, 1993.

Rice, Eve. *Benny Bakes a Cake.* New York: Greenwillow, 1981.

____. *Sam, Who Never Forgets.* New York: Greenwillow, 1977.

Rockwell, Anne and Harlow. *The First Snowfall.* New York: Macmillan, 1987.

Sierra, Judy. *The Flannel Board Storytelling Book.* New York: H. W. Wilson, 1987.

Silverstein, Shel. *The Giving Tree.* New York: Harper and Row, 1964.

____. *Where the Sidewalk Ends.* New York: Harper and Row, 1974.

Spier, Peter. *Dreams.* New York: Doubleday, 1986.

____. *Rain.* Garden City, N.Y.: Doubleday, 1982.

Staines, Bill. *All God's Critters Got a Place in the Choir.* Illustrated by Margot Zemach. New York: Dutton, 1989.

Bibliography

Tafuri, Nancy. *Have You Seen My Duckling?* New York: Greenwillow, 1984.

Talbot, Hudson. *We're Back.* New York: Crown, 1987.

Tashjian, Virginia A. *With a Deep Sea Smile: Story Stretches for Large or Small Groups.* Illustrated by Rosemary Wells. Boston: Little, Brown, 1974.

Waber, Bernard. *Ira Says Goodbye.* Boston: Houghton Mifflin, 1988.

Walsh, Ellen Stoll. *Mouse Paint.* San Diego: Harcourt Brace Jovanovich, 1989.

Watanabe, Shigeo. *How Do I Put It On?* New York: Philomel, 1979.

Westcott, Nadine Bernice. *I Know an Old Lady Who Swallowed a Fly.* Boston: Little, Brown, 1980.

Wiesner, David. *Tuesday.* New York: Clarion, 1991.

Wilmes, Liz and Dick. *Felt Board Fun.* Illustrated by Donna Dane. Dundee, Ill.: Building Blocks, 1984.

For further reading about children's musical recordings, check out the following books.

Jarnow, Jill. *All Ears: How to Choose and Use Recorded Music for Children.* New York: Penguin Books, 1991.

Sale, Laurie. *Growing Up with Music: A Guide to the Best Recorded Music for Children.* New York: Avon Books, 1992.

♪♩ *Index of Song Titles* ♩♪

Index of Song Titles

Index of Song Titles

Currently children's librarian at the L. E. Phillips Memorial Public Library in Eau Claire, Wisconsin, Rob Reid received a master's degree in library science from the University of Minnesota in 1984. He is the author of *The Goodbye Rap,* a picture book to be published by Lee & Low Books in 1996. Reid also reviews children's recorded music for *School Library Journal* and writes children's music and story programming columns for various newspapers and periodicals.